PeopleSoft HRMS Interview Questions, Answers, and Explanations

ORACOOKBOOK.COM

TABLE OF CONTENTS

PeopleSoft HRMS Interview Questions, Answers, and Explanations

ORACOOKBOOK
Equity Press

☞ QUESTION 1

Adding a new SS transaction in MSS

The business need is to create a new transaction on MSS so that the managers can give ad hoc stock awards to their team. Currently using variable compensation, it can be achieved but with complications. The security that exists in MSS does not exist in Variable Compensation. That is purely delivered from an administrative stand point.

Is it possible to add any new self service transactions on E-Profile Manager Desktop?

How difficult is it to add a new self service transaction on MSS?

✍ ANSWER

Your objective is not a trivial effort. If you need approval functionality, it gets even more complex. I did the mod back in 8.3 SP1 and it took about a month to design code and test each transaction. Unless you are very familiar with the direct reports frame-work, the computer interfaces, workflow, role queries and advanced component processing, I would think twice about doing this kind of modification.

☞ QUESTION 2

Difference and Upgrade of Security in HRMS 8.9

Are there documents that explain the differences between security in HRMS 8.3 and HRMS 8.9?

What is the difference in Security when moving from PeopleTools 8.1 xs to 8.46?

✍ ANSWER

Security in v8.9 HCM has made a few changes. I would suggest starting with the white paper that PeopleSoft has posted on peoplesoft.com (search for 8.9 security white paper). That should help identify the overall changes.

Oracle also published a Red Paper in August of 2005 "Enterprise HRMS Row Level Security in 8.9", and a Red Paper on Person Model as well. Both are must reads.

To give you a general idea, the main change is an ability to secure on data that isn't DEPTID. Since the new person model allows records to be stored without a job record (and therefore without a DEPTID), there had to be some changes to secure records with no JOB on a basis other than DEPTID. This applies across the whole system, and is useful for jobs where DEPTID security isn't desirable.

To visualize it more, let me give you a sample implementation. There was a project developed that has a custom security set that implemented row level security by region for 'People with Jobs'. A sibling table was created to the department table with one of four regions attached to each department. The SJT SQL that was required was written for the fast security tables and created the required permission lists and roles to implement. HCM 8.9 has many more options than even 8.8 when it comes to row level security. It is much more flexible, and requires much less work to customize. There wasn't a business need to use any of the POI functionality, but 'Person of Interest' gives even more flexibility within the same frame-work.

☞ QUESTION 3

Missing Employee ID value on PS_APPLICANT

I am using PeopleTools 8.45. I've noticed that there's a bug in the recruitment of internal applicants. There are some applicants whose employee ID's are null on application data page. The APPLID and EMPLID value on that page should always be equal.

Do you have any idea on why some applicants have a missing employee ID value on the page?

✍ ANSWER

Employee ID is not required on the PS applicant. You can load many internal applicants without employee ID's and you can fetch them programmatically. However, if you are using the delivered employee home module and require the internal applicant to log in, the employee ID should populate on the applicant record first.

☞ QUESTION 4

Converting EMP to CWR in HR8.9

We have a situation here due to improper data entry.

1. A contingent worker has been entered as an employee into the system with PER_ORG as EMP. In order to control other things, we made this payroll and benefits system other than PS. We do not pay contingent workers out of PeopleSoft HR. We just keep their personal and job info.

   Now we need to change this PER_ORG into CWR. Is there a better way to change this through PIA rather than through the back end? One way I can think of is to terminate the employee and then re-hire the contingent worker in to the system. If we use the same employee ID the system might give him an employee record of 1 which the users do not want. Can you suggest a good and efficient procedure just in case this happens again?

2. The users, when adding a person as organization entered an employee record of 999. This logically should be 0, as we do not have a concept of multiple jobs. Most of the interfaces and batch processes have this file hard coding to Zero. Other than a backend method, can we change this to zero? Is there an efficient way of avoiding this in the future?

I previously planned to make that field display only on the page so that users cannot change the value.

✍ ANSWER

If he's never been paid under the old ID, use the delete ID process and start over. However if there is history on that id, you cannot do that.

An alternative would be to use the Archive Data Tool. Do a manual update on changing the Value of PER_ORG field from EMP to CWR.

☞ QUESTION 5

Contingent Workers in PS 8.9

"The employee and contingent worker relationship represent your workforce and are the main focus of the business processes in Enterprise HCM. Most of the processes that are designed for employees are also available for contingent workers with the following exceptions:

- Payroll for North America
- Plan Salary
- Plan Careers and Successions
- Variable Compensation"

The notation above is from the Red Paper on Person Model.

In our company we have decided not to use contingent workers and stick with 'employees' and 'persons of interests without jobs' as the organizational relationships. However, some of the fields in the JOB component might be helpful for recording POI information.

If you have Payroll for NA and are using Contingent Workers, how could this be utilized? How do you fill out required data fields in the JOB component?

✍ ANSWER

When you add a contingent worker on JOB record, mention that the Payroll System is maintained outside PeopleSoft.

Just to be on the safe side I would also create a separate pay group for these folks. Assign them so there is no way they would be included in your normal pay run. The organizational type of contingent worker really should do the trick. Better safe than sorry.

In PS Books there is a one line reference regarding Contingent Workers not be paid from NA Payroll.

☞ QUESTION 6

Add new action on Job data page

We are using PeopleSoft HCM 8.8, PeopleTools 8.45, and Oracle database. Our client faces a unique situation where the employee agrees to join but later drops out. In the mean time, to complete his joining formalities the applicant's employee ID has already been created. So the client wants to take a suitable action on the job data page. The employee should be inactivated on taking this particular action. An employee's status becomes inactive when he is terminated.

How can we similarly inactivate the status of the employee when we take this newly added action 'Drop Out'?

Is it advisable to add a new action that inactivates the employee status?

What are the future dependencies on creating such new actions?

✍ ANSWER

Adding new action or reasons with behavior to Terminate or Inactivate requires customization of PeopleCode that you may not want to perform.

An option would be to take an existing action or reason that does inactivate that "employee", instead of a new one. If it's an exceptional situation, an exceptional measure is ok.

You could even delete the complete employee. There is an employee deletion tool in the Setup HRMS / System Admin / Database Processes. In that case it may not be really necessary to keep that "employee" file in the HRMS database. He was never an employee after all.

From a best practices perspective, my recommendation is that you terminate the "employee" with an action term or reason "Did Not Start". That way you can achieve the result of inactivating the employee and have a record of the job, reason and metrics, if you want to report these. Adding reasons would be relatively easy.

☞ **QUESTION 7**

COMBO CODE Set Up

HCM v8.9 now uses two tables, a new PS_VALID_COMBO_CODE and the old PS_ACCT_CD_TBL.

It unclear how maintenance on these tables should be performed in the future when new combo codes are added.

Online, the user will be populating PS_VALID_COMBO_CODE, and yet most of the T&L module is still using PS_ACCT_CD_TBL for field validation.

So how does the user enter COMBO CODES that can be used?

✍ **ANSWER**

There are processes that can be setup via applied messaging to be loaded and maintained through the FIN system, but the applied messages need to be in place. The non commitment accounting tables have even more changes and more new tables that need to be setup manually or through a custom process. Commitment accounting can share with FIN thru applied messaging.

☞ QUESTION 8

ID assignment at the top of the chain?

We are a little perplexed whether we should designate the Supervisor ID for our CEO/President. He technically reports to the Board of the Directors. We are currently running PS 8.9 with Mgr SS, and I'm afraid that if we indicate the Supervisor ID as the CEO's that this will cause a vicious loop in processing (especially regarding MSS processing) by having him report to himself.

Are these reservations warranted? Is there a work around to this reporting relationship cycle?

✍ ANSWER

There is nothing wrong with having the CEO's Supervisor ID report to himself.

An alternative you could use if you are on 8.8 to 8.9 is to have the SUPERVISOR_ID blank for all employees. Then use the REPORTS_TO filed and the top person's (owner) field blank as well.

For what I recall when studying Trees a few versions ago, all departments have to report to another department except for the top one, who reports to itself.

☞ QUESTION 9

Code dynamic prompt tables on the MSS HCM 8.9 for LOA

Since PeopleSoft does not provide Leave of Absence functionality on MSS, I went forward and added a few more action reasons on the Termination page so that the Managers can use this page for both Termination and LOA purposes. However, the requirement now is that once the manager selects an ACTION on the page, then the idea is to show those ACTION REASONS associated with that ACTION only so as to avoid confusion.

Ideally once the user enters the ACTION, then the prompt table for the ACTION REASON field should dynamically change and look at the right prompt table.

How can I achieve this?

✍ ANSWER

If you look on JOB this is done automatically and you don't have to assign anything dynamically. PeopleSoft handles it just by the keys.

But in case you want to change the prompt table dynamically you use the derived record and use any of the editable fields. Place the editable field on the page and use the code assign to prompt the table dynamically.

Something like this should appear: "&this_RECNAMEEDIT2 = "POSN_JOB_UPD".

☞ QUESTION 10

PeopleSoft Global Payroll Country Extension Payroll Calculation

PeopleSoft Global Payroll Country extension 8.9 for Australia or Malaysia:

1. The Payroll and Absence calculation rule PS delivered for that specific country statutory requirement, would provide the element owner, type of "PS Delivered and Maintained" for that specific country.   From the DEMO, I could only find the element owner type of "PS Delivered and Not Maintained".   In one article, I saw that PS promised to deliver the statutory rule for that specific country on the country extension product.

   Is this always the case or sometimes only support the element owner type of 'PS Delivered and Not Maintained" for that specific country?

2. For off cycle process, does the PS deliver any seeded element for that specific country extension like Hong Kong, Malaysia, or Japan?

✍ ANSWER

There are two basic types of "OWNER" for any Global Payroll element. One is "Customer", and the other is "PS".

Within the "PS" option there are four variations:

- M PS Delivered/Customer Modified
- N PS Delivered / Not Maintained
- P PS Delivered / Maintained
- S PS Delivered/Maintained/Secure

The core of Global Payroll will have some elements for each of these four variations plus some "Customer" within the DEMO database. Each Country Extension will then have additional elements in each of these four groups.

To see what you have in any database you can use the following query made for the MSSQL server.

SELECT COUNT (PIN_NUM), PIN_OWNER
FROM PS_GP_PIN
WHERE PIN_OWNER <> 'C'
GROUP BY PIN_OWNER
ORDER BY 2

In Mexico, this is the result:

10 M
1,035 N
1,002 P
720 S

☞ QUESTION 11

Calling PeopleSoft page from non-PeopleSoft page

How can I call a PeopleSoft page from a Non-PeopleSoft page, supposing the Non-PeopleSoft page to be VB?

Is it by component interface or are there other means?

✍ ANSWER

It depends upon your requirement. From a non-PeopleSoft page like a VB page, VB just serves as a client server technology with ASP as an extended version which extends VB to the Internet Browser.

Presuming you have ASP application which needs to make a call to PeopleSoft, there are different techniques. You can create a link in a JSP application which takes you to PeopleSoft with a "Single Sign On" enabled. The actor will then perform some activities and then return back to ASP application carrying data in a Computer Interface (CI) object.

☞ QUESTION 12

Steps involved in conversion during implementation

What are the steps involved in conversion from the mainframes during an implementation of HRMS?

✍ ANSWER

You can do the following steps:

1. Extract the data from the mainframe.
2. Insert the data into PeopleSoft.

Note: There might be a need for some type of transformation of data between Steps 1 and 2.

☞ QUESTION 13

Remote Call error

We are suddenly getting the following error when trying to calculate an online check:

"Unable to initiate Remote Call. User does not have write permission to directory c:\Peoplesoft8App\HR822P\ Appserv\HRSYS8\logs (2,-1) At FUNCLIB_UTIL.RC_TEST_ PBFieldChange PCPC: 2655 Statement: 26"

We've checked the permission and they haven't changed. The users should have permission to write to the folder.

How can we resolve this?

✍ ANSWER

Check if the disk space is full. You can also try to delete the redundant message in the folder.

If the above does not work, try a test using the remote call test utility. If that also fails then it may be a COBOL configuration issue. If this is the problem, copy the COBOL's from the UNIX server to Application server.

Other alternatives would be to check the single "Check functionality" and the remote call test utility.

☞ QUESTION 14

Joining 2 tables

There's this requirement for me to create a query where I have to pull the information from PS_PAY_CHECK table and join it with a table in ERNCD field.

I'll be using these two tables to pull and get the sum of the total gross for a given employee on a given ERNCD.

How can I find the right table in ERNCD for this task?

✍ ANSWER

There is an approach you can use to solve these kinds of problems. You need to have access to PeopleTools. If not, get someone with access to help you follow the following procedure:

1. Open the field ERNCD.
2. Find Object References for the ERNCD field.
3. Tools will return all the record names (and other objects) containing ERNCD field.
4. Search for likely candidates. Open the record PAY_ CHECK and note the key fields. Any record to be joined will need to have one or more of the key fields.
5. Open likely candidate records and check the key fields. Check the relationship between PAY_CHECK and this record. Develop the JOIN criteria based on the relationship.

Sometimes it helps to look at some rows of data in each of the tables to see if things are going to work out. Suggestions: PAY_EARNINGS and PAY_OTH_EARNS would be your choice. You cannot use ERNCD filed to join these, as PAY_CHECK tables' does not have this field in it. You should understand the requirement first.

Pay Earnings table does not contain EMPLID. It has page number and Line Number. PAY CHECK number has all three, and that's the reason they asked you to pull the info using PAY CHECK.

☞ QUESTION 15

Check Print

What are the SQR's that needs to be modified when changing the Check Printers?

My requirement is having the signature plates be replaced. What are the things that need to be changed?

The old printer was a LEXMARK and the new one is the HP LASERJET 4250 (TROY and Standard Register Software).

On analysis, I found that the old printer uses linkup software between the PeopleSoft and the printer. The new printer does not use any link up software.

For the new printer, the person who installed it says that the Signatures and Logos were installed on a Flash Card in a public file mode and the MICR and secure amount were installed in secure mode.

The thing we discovered is on the logo and the signature that prints the PITCH and POINT match. On the logo and the signature that does not print, the PITCH and POINT do not match

On the MICR, the Standard Register support is saying that we need to un-secure the MICR code.

How do I fix both these issues?

✍ ANSWER

There is nothing to change in the SQR. Check with PS if the new printer is certified. If your signature is on the chip then you have to buy another one for the new printer.

There are no changes to be made to the programs (PAY003 or DDP003). This is true if you are using soft font loading of MICR and a bmp file of the signature.
However, if either of your MICR and signatures (or logos) are imbedded in a SIMM/DIMM chip and this chip is new, then make sure you got the right PCL codes from whoever created your chip.

Characters are imbedded in a chip and located in areas called grids. You need to know where in the grid they are located. This is the only change that you have to do in PAY003.

If however you are just moving the old chip into the new printer then there is nothing to change assuming that the chip is compatible with the new printer.

Here's an example of a chip that has two signatures:

Encode '<27>&f102y0x0S<27>(4B<27>(s0p3h12v0s0b102T' into $SigFont1 !;
Encode '<27>&f103y0x0S<27>(4C<27>(s0p3h12v0s0b103T' into $SigFont2 !;
Encode '<27>&f1s0S<27>&a+000V<33><34><35><36><37> <38><39><40><41><42> into $SigLine1;
Encode '<27>&f1s0S<27>&a+120V<43><44><45><46><47> <48><49><50><51><52> into $SigLine2
Encode '<27>&f1s0S<27>&a+240V<53><54><55><56><57> <58><59><60><61><62> into $SigLine3;
Encode '<27>&f1s0S<27>&a+360V<63><64><65><66><67>

<68><69><70><71><72> into $SigLine4;
Encode '<27>&f1s1x3x8X' into $SigTail;

As for the MICR, just turn it ON using PCL command just before printing the MICR. You don't need to turn it OFF since it will auto off at the end of the program. Here's how to turn it OFF:

Encode '<27><27>%-12400X' into $micr_command;
Print $micr_command () code;

☞ QUESTION 16

Deleting dependent info of an employee

How do I delete dependent information of an employee who has only one dependent?

✍ ANSWER

Look in 8.9 HRMS. Go the ERD diagrams to see where dependant data is stored and write SQL to delete them.

There are 6 main tables on HR8.9 to delete the dependents, DEP_BEN, DEP_NID, etc. Make sure you also remove them from the HEALTH_DEPENDENT table if they have a row for it.

If you are on PeopleTools 8.46, it has a tool called "Find Data" under Archive Data Menu to assist you further in the task.

☞ **QUESTION 17**

Processes in HCM 8.9

Where can I find the list of all batch processes that a client has to run once they go live with HCM 8.9 with modules HR, Base Benefits, North American Payroll, ePay and eProfile (Vanilla System)?

✎ **ANSWER**

Where can I find the list of all batch processes that a client has to run once they go live with HCM 8.9 with modules HR, Base Benefits, North American Payroll, ePay and eProfile (Vanilla System)?

☞ QUESTION 18

Competency Management 8.9

I am unable to see search results using perform competency search components in PS HRMS 8.9, even though there are employees in database satisfying the search criteria. An example is provided below:

"Navigation: Workforce Development>Competency Management>Perform Competency Search > Search All"

How can I get this functionality working?

✍ ANSWER

You need to set the evaluation types for your user ID.

Use this:

"Workforce Development>Competency Management>Match Competences to roles> match evaluation types";

Afterwards, find your user ID

Select competency search in search type, and then add the evaluation types you want to use for searches.

☞ QUESTION 19

Handling 401K % change of 0 in PSFT 8.9 to pass to ADP

We are currently on PSFT HRMS 8.9 and we use ADP for our payroll processing. We have a scenario where an employee changed his 401k contribution from 5% to 0%. Since he changed it to 0% the ADP setup is no longer picking this employee record due as ADP still has the previous record of 5% and his deduction is continuing.

When we contacted PSFT they said they don't have an immediate solution. This is a common scenario

A second scenario: An employee changed his 401k contribution from 5% to 0% and since it is 0, I guess the file that is generated from PeopleSoft is no longer picking this employee information since it is considering that he is not enrolled in the 401k program. ADP still has the old record and is still deducting 5%.

How do I resolve these issues?

✍ ANSWER

Normally a 0 deduction in payroll interface would produce a stop record (tilde) which would delete the deduction record in ADP. 401k stops don't seem to work the same way.

Actually 401k stops are not something employees do throughout the year except for terms. Usually it's done upon hire, term, or a new benefit election year. Changes from one percent to another will be included in the file. It's only the "stops" that do not work.

As a workaround, create a user query that identified 401k election terminations. This would mean that you would create a benefit termination record for the 401k election. Run the query each period and then do the maintenance manually in ADP. For a company with approximately 1000 employees this resulted in about 1-2 entries per month.

An alternative solution will be to write an SQR that goes with the ADP process that will read the output excel file and accordingly will identify the employees with 0 deductions and place a ~.

☞ QUESTION 20

Reversal/Adjustments after Pay Cycle Closed to Off-Cycles

What do I do in the event of a need to do a reversal or a reversal adjustment to an employee's check after that pay run has been closed to off-cycle runs?

Example: Pay Run A has created a pay check for an employee that either needs to be reversed or adjusted. The pay is confirmed but the need for the reversal or adjustment is not noticed at that time.

Next Pay Run B is processed and confirmed. The confirmation process then closes Pay Run A to any off-cycle pays. At this time the need for the reversal or adjustment of the check created in Pay Run A is noticed, but now Pay Run is closed to off-cycle processing.

At this point, how can the check from Pay Run A which is in error be processed through the Reversal/Adjustment process?

If I go to the reversal/adjustment run control page, the pay end date of Pay Run A is no longer available for input on the Run Control.

How can this be fixed?

✍ ANSWER

You have two choices:

1) Create a new pay run for year end (use 12/31/05 as pay period begin, end, and check date) - make this an off cycle run. Reverse the check and it attaches itself to the next off cycle run available. Confirm the year end pay run and you should all be set.

2) If you don't want to create a new pay run or you already closed pay calendar that uses 12/31 as pay end dt, then you can do balance adjustments for all buckets (balances) that appeared on the check. This is a little trickier because you not only have to do the earnings and deductions, but also both sides of taxes and taxable wage buckets as well.

☞ **QUESTION 21**

Programs to insert new hire

Are there programs that insert new hire information into PS. 8.x?

✍ **ANSWER**

Yes there are. There are companies running few batch processes to automatically enroll new hire into some benefit programs. These same programs do some processing which will add new rows to a lot of tables, making the users work easier.

For example:

A restaurant company hires hourly employees using an interface from the time clock at the restaurant, first to a home-grown database where W4 information is added along with other HR functions such as Term Reason, then uploaded into PeopleSoft. They hire about 85 people a week, and term just as many, and all this is done in about 10 minutes with some help from the managers at the restaurants.

It is not without its user issues but you will find that every possible little problem can not be programmed in. You need to constantly tweak the interface but it beats hiring a staff to do the hiring and terming.

☞ QUESTION 22

Changing home and mailing address self-service

My client would like to modify the 'Home and Mailing Address' component in the eProfile self-service module to become 'Home and Other Address'.

The address page only shows 'Home and Mailing' address rows, regardless of the other addresses rows that can be used on that employee file. There is also logic to only allow adding 'Home' if you only have 'Mailing' address.

However, I carefully reviewed the component, all PeopleCode component, and records, functions calls, etc. through PeopleCode debugger. I can't figure out how this filtering is done when the page data is loaded. T here are no scroll select, and no view criteria to match those types.

The only thing I found is the HR_HOME_MAILING page activate PeopleCode, where you can find, among other stuff:

Component AddressCollection &AddrColl;
Component AddrSummaryControl &AddrSmryControl;

&Level1 = GetLevel0 () (1).GetRowset(Scroll.PERSON_ADDRESS);
&AddrColl = create AddressCollection(&Level1);
&AddrColl.EmployeeId = HR_SS_PERS_SRCH.EMPLID.Value;
&AddrSmryControl = create AddrSummaryControl();

&AddrSmryControl.fAddValues = GetLevel0 () (1).
DERIVED_CO.ADDR_TYPE_DESCR;
&AddrSmryControl.rsData = &AddrColl;
&AddrSmryControl.InitDisplay();

What are the functions of these?

If it's dynamic, do I need to use some parameters in the Setup?

✍ ANSWER

There is a way around this. Go to the Address Type set up page. Delete the MAIL row. Then insert a row and put it back in, use a code of MAIL but use your own descriptions. This will change some of the page headings in self service. If that's not enough, the remaining headings might be easier to change.

It's all about application package CO_ADDRESS that uses the magic view ADDRESS_TYP_SS that dynamically drives the whole process.

Modify the view and you have proper filtering and the drop down list of address type updated is automatically in the self-service page.

☞ QUESTION 23

Difference between HCM 8.8 and 8.9

What are the differences between HCM 8.8 and 8.9?

✍ ANSWER

The biggest difference is the new "Person" model. This will change the way employees are entered and stored. Prior to v8.9 the hire process required both personal and job data to be entered prior to assigning an employee ID. In v8.9 once the personal data component is entered you can enter and save the "person". They are not considered as an employee until you add the employment instance.

Another big change is redesigned security.

There is a white paper on customer connection that details the security changes.

There are also some navigation changes, but not as drastic as the changes from 8.3 to 8.8.

☞ QUESTION 24

Hide a text field in PeopleCode

Is it possible to hide and unhide a text field on a page using PeopleCode?

Is it possible to manipulate controls that are not part of a record?

✍ ANSWER

In PeopleCode, you have controls on fields and group box, but not text fields.

You could replace the text object by a derived field and set the text in it with PeopleCode under the conditions you need.

☞ QUESTION 25

Alpha-Numeric Employee ID

Currently, we employ a character (5) employee ID but we only use digits. We face an issue of running out of employee IDs in the near future under this numeric digit character (5) employee ID scheme. I was wondering if anyone ever considered or implemented an alpha-numeric employee ID scheme and what problems, issues, special considerations were encountered using these?

We could just keep it numeric and just increase the size but that may be more invasive as all the code/routines/procedures/etc. would have to be researched and modified if there is a dependency or logic locked into a 5 character coding scheme. Whereas it might be less invasive if you just keep it a size of five. On the other hand, if I introduce letters into the coding scheme, I thought it might boost the available supply of IDs.

What are my options here and how do I get ahead of the situation before a serious shortage of IDs happens?

✍ ANSWER

Employee ID in PeopleSoft goes all the way thru all tables with consistency. Since Employee ID is a character field, then its usage really is up to you. You may have to question your policy why only 5 characters are being used.

The problem lies with your customized programs. You may have to review the usage with your tech people.

In all of the programs, it does not really matter if the value is 5 characters or not. We simply use the field's property as vanilla as possible.

If you are using auto assigning employee ID, use all numbers as a precaution or preparation for future expansion and user needs.

☞ QUESTION 26

Payroll Balance Adjustments

I have a situation where one of the employees was overpaid in January 2005.

The employee has issued a manual check to the company for the over payment amount. The employee was terminated.

How do I reflect this in PeopleSoft?

✍ ANSWER

The solution depends on how the employee was paid. If it was paid to them via paper check, you can reverse (void) the check in PeopleSoft Reversal page; if not, you can do balance adjustments for all earnings, deductions, taxes that were reflected on the original payment. Remember if you adjust a tax balance, you also need to adjust the taxable wage amount as well.

☞ QUESTION 27

Security in talent acquisition manager 8.9

I'm looking for information on how security is applied across this module.

My specific questions are:

- How is access restricted to applicants?

- How is access restricted to job openings?

Take note that when a job opening is created it remains in a limited pool for a while before being public and accessible to all recruiters.

Is there a way to manage 2 pools for both applicants and job openings?

✍ ANSWER

In relation to the access for external applicants, there is a default role provided in PeopleSoft for them.

In the case of Job Openings, if you want to restrict job openings you should go for row level security in the set up HRMS.

☞ QUESTION 28

Grossing Up

The management has given each employee at one of our sites a $5.00 gift card from Blockbuster. This was nice but unfortunately IRS wants some of that. We now have a new earnings code and a new deduction code we gross up for taxes so the net amount of the check is 0 but the taxes are recorded.

We have keyed app. 400 of these as off cycle checks. Each represenative typed a new pay sheet form, (10 is the maximum per paysheet form) then they keyed on the paysheet in People Soft. The checks were calculated & confirmed, then printed. It looks like we might have over 400 more to do.

Is there anyway that we could make this an easier process? It took us about 42 man hours to do 400.

Does PeopleSoft have a pre-programmed way of entering 400 entries with gross, up to the pay sheets?

✍ ANSWER

This is what we commonly call as mass loading. If the earnings are all equal to all employees then you can just create an SQR to load into pay_other_earns table for each employee. If the amount varies by employee then you can use an excel file then mass upload to the same table.

The only difference in what we are doing is that this mass upload happens on a regular pay cycle and not as an off cycle checks. You would only use off cycle check for those immediate needs like terminations.

☞ QUESTION 29

Regular Workflow Settings in Marital status change

There is a business flow defined for marital status change in the BusinessProcess HR_SS_Work_Events. Within the process there is an activity for Marital Status change where a mail notification is defined. I need to change the mail content. When I click the mail notification it shows me Field mapping, where mail & note text are defined as REC Field.

Where can I find the mail content for that particular notification?

Is it in the front end?

✍ ANSWER

Search for record.field (mentioned in workflow field mapping) in your component, record, page PeopleCode. All you need to do is modify that PeopleCode to use your new text.

☞ QUESTION 30

Importing merit raise data into PeopleSoft

I am working on an SQR to import merit raise data into PeopleSoft HRMS 8.80.01.000. I am using a program that was used to do the same into ADP Enterprise. It inserts into PS_JOB a new effective dated row with the emplid, rec nbr, action reason, new comprate, change amt, change percent, annual monthly and hourly rates.

In PeopleSoft, is there any other record that needs to be updated?

Are there processes to berun after importing the data?

✍ ANSWER

Run it through CI in order for PeopleCode to fire.

If you enter a row in PS_JOB, then you also need to enter a row in PS_COMPENSATION and PS_JOBJR. These 3 tables should have the same number of rows, with the same effective dates in sync.

Once you load these tables, you can run the Calculate compensation process, which is in Workforce administration > Job data.

This should take care of everything. By doing this you can avoid writing a CI (Component Interface).

About your amounts, you can enter only Annual Salary for

salaried people and hourly rate for hourly employees and the 'calculate compensation process" takes care of the rest.

Make sure you populate the above three tables mentioned.

☞ QUESTION 31

Job data change error

Here is an error that I encounter:

"Changes conflict with another data item (18, 5)".

We are using HRMS 8.3. This happens while inserting a row to job data and save application.

How do I resolve this?

✍ ANSWER

Look to see if there is a future dated row. That's one possible culprit. Then there's the infamous correction mode. There are instances when a change has been made in correction mode and not all the tables get changed, like the BAS Activity table. When you insert a new row, it's in conflict with another row that wasn't changed.

☞ QUESTION 32

Push Button appears enabled to some, disabled to others

A while ago I created a page intended for uploading and downloading attachments. It has come to my attention that when opening attachments, the "Open" button appears enabled to some people and disabled to others. The only code that controls this property checks if the filename is empty or not:

If MYRECORD.FILENAME = "" Then
Gray (MYRECORD.VIEWATTBTN);
End-If

Is the "enabled" property also affected by row security or anything like it?

✍ ANSWER

There's a property that indicates if the push-button should also be enabled when the page is 'Display only'. It can be found in the Page Field Properties page for the push-button in Application Designer. This is why some people have the button enabled and some don't. It was a permissions issue with the page having full access or being Display Only.

☞ QUESTION 33

Delete an EMPLID from all tables

I need to delete an EMPLID from all tables used by New Hire. This is a Test EMPLID that was accidentally hired into Production instead of Test.

"Delete ID" can't trace the person, but doing SQL Query found him in JOB, PERSONAL_DATA, and COMPENSATION.

Where else should I look?

✍ ANSWER

Write an SQR that will scrutinize PSRECFIELD. Select only table_names where it has field EMPLID then use the table_names to delete the employee record.

Search the PeopleCode behind it to find other records that may contain that EMPLID.

Afterwards, delete them with SQL and double check other records.

☞ QUESTION 34

Session Administration in 8.3 for Training Module

How do I conduct sessions that can span multiple days?

Example:

A class runs for two consecutive days between 8-5. What do I use as start/end dates and times, and what is the duration in terms of days, hours, etc?

Or a class runs for two days and then weeks apart Monday 10/5 and Monday 10/19 again. How do you enter that into session administration?

✍ ANSWER

There aren't any perfect solutions. You do it differently depending on the course and the audience. For some you set each day up as a separate session and require the attendee to enroll in each one. For others, just put it in as one session, the number of hours for the course (all sessions) in the duration and then spell out what the dates and times are in the Course Content on the last page of the Course table. Even though it is a hassle to make people enroll for each session, it does make tracking of who comes, and who doesn't, easier.

☞ QUESTION **35**

HR Service Centers

I need some information about established HR service centers.

What were the things that worked well? What were the things that did not work so well? How did you address staffing size and mix? What tasks did the SC perform? What sort of change management did you perform during transition? What metrics and measures were in place before and how did they improve afterwards?

✍ ANSWER

There will always be loads of arguments about what transactions should be moved into the service center. It depends a lot on whether you mean an outsourced service center or an internal one. The biggest change or challenge is often simply giving the service center staff the power to say "no". They need this backing from the very top or all the good work you've pushed out creeps back into the service center and the model fails.

☞ QUESTION 36

PS 8.9 Person Model

We are looking to upgrade to 8.9 (or done so already) and might opt to use the new "person model". I would like to know what could be the impact and if the person model is strictly HRMS or does it have implications across other modules?

✍ ANSWER

In v8.9 you don't have the option. The Person Model is the only option for the HRMS system. The main difference is that the Person and Job records are entered, maintained, and stored separately. Contingent workers and/or Person of Interests (POI) are stored with an "Emplid" and are stored with a different type in the same way the Person records are stored. It can be saved without the job record.

It can affect your reports and queries if you don't add the correct criteria of whether to include or exclude the "non employee" types.

It also affects security; you have to create permissions for employees with jobs and/or employees without jobs.

☞ QUESTION 37

Set up action for retro pay

In retroactive pay, how do we set up retroactive pay to trigger on events from job data?

✍ ANSWER

When you are running the Retro Pay Calculation process, you select which processes you want to trigger the calculation. There are check boxes for Job and/or additional pay. This is where you tell it what type of actions will trigger the retro pay process. You have to have the retro pay programs already setup but the Job Action trigger occurs from the Processing page.

☞ QUESTION 38

Row-level security: view rows from same department

I'm trying to implement row level security in my PeopleSoft implementation. However, I'm not quite sure where to start. I would like a certain operator to be able to view only the rows that correspond to his/her department. Do I create a permission list?

Is it possible to assign row-level security to:

1. A single operator?
2. A role?
3. A permission list?

I know there's row level security in which all operators can only view the data in their own business unit. Sometimes it is necessary to have some users view ALL data and some users view data within their own department. Is this possible? If so, how is it done?

✍ ANSWER

First you create an empty permission list and name it DP%. You can do this in:

Home->PeopleTools->Maintain Security->Use->Permission Lists

Then you go to:

Home->Define Business Rules->Administer HR System->Use->Maintain Row Level Security;

Here you pick the permission list you created in the first step. Then you select the SetID, DeptID and Access Code (Read/Write or No Access permissions). Save this. Now you have a permission list which grants access to rows from a certain SetID and DeptId only.

Finally, you must add this permission list to the user profiles. To do this, go to:

Home->PeopleTools->Maintain Security->Use->User Profiles;

Pick the user profile and in the "Row Security" edit box, and type the name of your permission list or click the prompt button to look for it. Save the User Profile and you're done!

☞ QUESTION 39

Crystal Reports Print Engine error text

When I am trying to run Crystal reports from "Administer Training/Report", I am getting the following error for some of the reports. Other crystals ran fine.

Error:
"Crystal Reports Print Engine error text: Error detected by database DLL"

How can I fix this?

✍ ANSWER

This error could be because one of the following reasons:

1. Check if the query exists in the database. You can query the PSQRYDEFN table.

2. There is a mismatch between the query and the Crystal report. To do this go into the Crystal Designer and use the option "Tools -> Verify Database". This will perform a sync check between the PS query and the crystal report and will synchronize the same.

3. The reason could be the parameters which you are passing through query as a prompt.

To resolve the problem, do the following:

1. In the process definition "Override Options" tab check the parameters list option and make it append and enter the parameters which you want to pass to process(ex crystal) from query.

Example:

ORIENTL: Run_cntl_tbl_name.parameter_name1

2. Restart the Process Scheduler service using the admin account
3. Then install workstation.

This should resolve the issue.

☞ QUESTION 40

Session timed out while entering new employee

Our HR administrator was hiring a new employee in PS when called away from her desk. Upon returning, her session had timed out. During this time, we used the requisition and applicant screens and they were completed. She had just entered the employee number in the hire area when she was called away and the session timed out.

When you view the applicant in the applicant screens, it indicated he is hired and shows the employee number. However, if you go to Job Data screens, it says the employee number doesn't exist.

I have tried reopening the job requirement, un-offering the job in the applicant section and starting over by tying the applicant to the requirement, offering and accepting in the applicant screens. When I try to "re-hire" the applicant and finish the screens, I get an error as follows:

"Data being added conflicts with existing data (18, 2); when adding a new item to the database, the system found a conflicting item already. This problem can happen if another user has entered similar information at the same time as you. Note the changes you have made, cancel the page, and then retry your changes.

If the problem persists, it may be because of an application or programming error and should be reported to technical staff. This error occurs when the keys on the record being inserted match a record that is already in the database. The application must ensure that each inserted record has unique keys."

We are on version 8.13 and I did not find the PERSON table.

How can I resolve this issue?

✍ ANSWER

If there is nothing in JOB this may not work, but try the Delete EMPLID function. I almost NEVER advise people to use it but in this case you should. Otherwise, that EMPLID will come up in searches and you don't want that to happen. There was no PERSON table in the version you are on. That comes later.

Try the 'Administer Workforce', Process and you should see Delete ID. Since you cannot see a JOB row for the EMPLID, there is a chance it will not work. Since it's going to be very difficult to replicate the problem in your test environment, I'd say give it a try. What's the worst thing that could happen? It doesn't work. In that case, I'd put DO NOT USE in the name field for the EMPLID and document it and let your users know. You should have trace running when you process the delete to see which tables are updated.

Of course, there is the old back-door method which you'll need a DBA for, and that's to delete the record from the tables. The problem with this is, you're not going to know what tables might have been populated.

☞ QUESTION 41

Unable to see the data Via PIA

We had our HR8.9 configurations done by PeopleSoft Lab and then we loaded all our HR tables via data conversion process. Now we are unable to see any of the employee information via PIA, but can see the data in the SQL query analyzer (backend).

The department tree was created by PeopleSoft and then we ran the Refresh transaction and SJT Classes. We are still unable to see any data.

✍ ANSWER

Before you run those processes make sure your JOB_JR table is populated, and then re-run those security admin processes.

Unless, and until you have data in SJT_PERSON AND SJT_ DEPT you cannot see the data via PIA. Please make sure your department tree is active in security sets and access pages.

Ensure the following things:

1. Navigate to Setup HRMS -> Security -> Core Row Level Security -> Security Set (see attachment for configuration) - make sure Department by Tree is enabled.

2. Setup HRMS -> Security -> Core Row Level Security ->

Security Access Type (see attachment for configuration) - again, make sure Department by Tree is enabled.

3. When you loaded JOB_JR, and you get any application engine error messages, make sure the field LASTUPDDTTM is blank or make the format to be YYYY-MM-DD.

4. Run Transaction SJT table refresh (Setup HRMS -> Security -> Core Row Level Security -> Refresh SJT transaction table (for ALL SECURITY SETS).

5. Run Refresh SJT Class table (Setup HRMS -> Security -> Core Row Level Security -> SJT_CLASS_ALL (delete the 'As of Date' for the Trees date).

6. Query SJT_PERSON & SJT_DEPARTMENT to make sure data is there.

☞ QUESTION 42

Recognizing fields behind a form in Lawson

We are implementing HR8.9 and currently converting from Lawson. We are in the phase of data conversion where we are bringing in all the data from Lawson into flat files and into PeopleSoft HR.

The major problem we have here is that no one from the Client side is there to technically work on Lawson. We do have access to the pages and forms in Lawson and can see what data is entered on the forms.

How does this data connect to the Records in the back end?

As in PS we hit CTRL J to see the page and open in the Application designer and get the record behind it. Is there a similar way in Lawson to do this?

✍ ANSWER

Lawson has a lot of similarities but also is very different from HR8.9. There are some tables that can help you with the conversion though.

The list of tables that will help you the most in data extraction from Lawson are as follows:

For HR:
　　1. EMPLOYEE
　　2. PAEMPLOYEE

3. PAEMERGCNT
4. HISTERR
5. HRHISTORY
6. HRSUPER
7. JOBCLASS
8. JOBCODE
9. PERSACTHST
10. PERSACTYPE

FOR BENEFITS:
1. BENEFICRY
2. BENEFIT
3. BNCATEGORY
4. BNCOVDFT
5. BNCOVERAGE
6. BNCOVOPT
7. BNPRMOPT
AND SOME BASIC INFO OF PAYROLL FROM:
1. PAREGISTER_PSOFT_VIEW1
2. PAYDEDUCTN_PSOFT_VIEW1
3. PAYMASTR_PSOFT_VIEW1

Payroll needs some understanding. It has a lot of tables and the field names are entirely different. For example, if you are looking for YTD, QTD amount field, you cannot find these in Lawson with that name. You find equivalent field names like WAGE_AMOUNT.

☞ QUESTION 43

Hiring discrepancy

How do you distinguish in PS HRMS when a person is hired, terminated, and then re-hired? Should the action in PS_JOB be 'HIR' for the second time? Should it be 'REH' or should it depend on the company that implements HRMS?

If he is hired back, should the EMPLID be different?

✍ ANSWER

I would imagine that you would be in all sorts of trouble if you have multiple HIR rows per employee. Furthermore, there is business logic that fires on a REH row to update rehire date in EMPLOYMENT etc. Use REH and get rid of your multiple HIR rows.

It is recommended to use rehire row, because when looking at benefits plans like STD an employee is counted on the number of service years where his previous employment also comes into consideration.

If you have a terminated employee with HR status Active, then you cannot add the same person with different employee in the HIRE row because there would be a conflict with the SSN number being the same.

☞ QUESTION 44

Increase size of field "Step" for Salary plan

We are using PeopleSoft HRMS 8.8, PeopleTools 8.45, and Oracle 9i database.

We have encountered a unique situation where we have more than 100 salary steps. Now the step field as provided by Peoplesoft takes a maximum of 2 digits. It has become inevitable that we increase the size of STEP field from 2 digits to 3 digits. As a result we will now have to alter around 157 records where this STEP field is used. Are there any repercussions that we may encounter because of this?

Can STEP take characters or if not, can it be modified to take characters?

✍ ANSWER

There will be plenty of repercussions. You will find it very difficult to maintain the changes that you have when you get updates from PeopleSoft.

What you can do is to submit your issues to PeopleSoft and force them to commit and implement an update. It would help to call other companies explain your issues and have them call PS. So far PS has been very good at complying with company's request. Remember, there is power in numbers.

☞ QUESTION 45

Processing Manual Benefit Program

I need to know where to look in resolving an error with BenAdmin. When we run PSPBARUN it gives the error:

'Can Not Process Manual Benefit Program' with the program name.

This is a manual benefit program and all employees in this plan have been terminated. However, there are a few who switched to an Automated Benefit program. Do the employees who switched need to be processed differently?

✍ ANSWER

After your initial enrollment, the only time you may change your benefit choices is during open enrollment or a qualified family status change.

The Info button provides you with additional information about your enrollment.

The Select button next to an event means it is currently open for enrollment.

To begin your enrollment, click Select.

Note: Some events may be temporarily closed until you have completed enrollment for a prior event

☞ QUESTION 46

Deleting Dependents

Can an employee delete his dependents through ebenefits?

Can the same employee add them when proof required is not selected?

✍ ANSWER

NO, an employee cannot delete his or her dependents through ebenefits.

EBenefits supports two Life Event transactions:

1. Marital Status Change - married / divorced.
2. Birth/Adoption.

The 'Proof required' works for these two life events only. 'Proof required' is nothing, but when you do not check this it means the changes are not updated in the database directly. Workflow comes in picture where it tells the Admin about the changes and then admin does the database update.

In the event of divorce, current spouse's marital status is changed to 'Divorced' and relationship is changed to 'Ex-Spouse in DEPENDENT_BENEF' table, but not deleted from the database.

I am talking of the Vanilla System. You can definitely customize it by giving permissions through security.

☞ QUESTION 47

Encryption of SSN in HR

Does PeopleSoft encrypt the SSN used in HR?

My client states this is a HUGE security issue including showing a masked version of the SSN online?

✍ ANSWER

I have never heard of it being encrypted, but that's on the Finance side when setting up employees as vendors.

I would think that the security requirements for SSN are no different for your entire DB. SSN doesn't need to be any more secure than the employee equity information, smoking status, salary information, bank account information, dependents, marital status, etc.

PeopleSoft certainly doesn't encrypt all the other details that could be used to thieve your identity, including bank account and personal information (at least not in 8.3 SP1). The only real encryption is password encryption. I'd say that you really need to manage your clients expectations, and at worst tell them that only a select few A/Ps and DBAs would have access to PRD data by scrambling all your staging environments. That should normally calm the IT auditors.

However, many companies are looking at the issue and as I recall there is a third party software company out there that does it. Here's the rub, many government documents, like garnishments and liens, are identified by SSN. As a matter of fact, you have to add the SSN as a search key to one of the pages in order for payroll to look things up with it. You may want to kindly inform them that they probably already have SSN floating around in other places they aren't even aware of.

While SSN is one of the more sensitive pieces of data, it is only one. It's going to be on your interfaces to your benefits carriers in many cases as that's the only way they have to uniquely identify your employees.

Advise your clients to take the number off any paper or process they can, including employee applications. Take it directly from the employee's SS card. Make the copy for the I-9 and then store it safely away.

☞ QUESTION 48

Help - HRIS Analyst Interview

What are common requirements for PeopleSoft HRMS positions?

What sort of experience will I need to land the job?

Example requirement:

This position serves as the Human Resources' resource on the HR/Payroll Systems Development and Implementation Team. The basic function is to supply the knowledge of Human Resources' policies, procedures, and processes to the tasks involved in implementing the various phases of PeopleSoft. This position recommends, and develops new processes and procedures necessary for successful implementation. The Sr. HRIS Analyst acts as a consultant to the HR division to identify and implement processes to enhance productivity and quality.

Responsibilities:

- Identify reports needed by the end-user departments. Write and produce PS Queries and SQL Plus Queries to provide the necessary standard and the ad-hoc reports required by the departments. Work with departments to continually enhance quality of reports developed, to ensure the highest possible productivity.
- Identify and manage security needs. Assist Information Protection and the requesting department in coordinating access needs and sensitivity of information.
- Maintain data integrity by validation of data input.
- Populate, maintain, and update the PS foundation and set-up tables. Assist Compensation and Payroll in maintaining/

updating PS tables identified in each department's are of responsibility.

- Communicate with internal and external contacts to stay current on system enhancements/upgrades, and to assist in resolving issues that arise in the development and maintenance of the PS • Maintain and enhance working knowledge of PeopleSoft and participate in User Group meetings.
- Provide end-user training. Maintain/update the end-user manual.
- Attend team meetings to identify project requirements, phases, work plans, and assist in resolving outstanding issues.
- Develop test plans for new releases, modifications and upgrades. Identify and direct the power-users needed to validate information and processing.

Requirements:

- Bachelor's Degree
- Minimum of four years experience working in HRIS and LAN environments, in such roles as: developer, report writer, end-user support, LAN management, or HRIS management.
- Two years experience with PeopleSoft, including the query-reporting tool.
- One-year experience with Cognos PowerPlay, preferred.
- Must be experienced with project planning developing unit and parallel testing, and gap reviews.
- Exceptional communication skills.
- Knowledge of and expertise with Windows and Microsoft Suite, specifically being proficient in the use of MS Word, Excel and MS PowerPoint.
- Working knowledge of, and expertise, utilizing and creating databases and spreadsheets.
- Experience in LAN utilization.
- Experience with creating, testing and performing QA,

queries and ad-hoc reports.
- Must be highly proficient in PeopleSoft query reporting tool.

✍ ANSWER

Without some PeopleSoft experience, it will be hard to land this position.

There really is no 2 to 3 day cram, but the information in this book will certainly help!

☞ QUESTION 49

Payroll Element Segmentation

I have Element Segmentation set up to segment earnings based on certain actions in JOB, including Termination and Rehire.

An employee was terminated with an effective date of January 14th 2005 and then rehired with an effective date of January 20th 2005.

When payroll was calculated his earnings were resolved to amounts in three slices:

Slice 1 - Jan 1st to Jan 13th
Slice 2 - Jan 14th to Jan 19th
Slice 3 - Jan 20th to Jan 31st

Should the earnings be calculated for the second slice, even though the payee is inactive for that slice period? If so, how do I get GP to resolve to zero for the second slice?

The Calendar is set up to process Active Payees Only. I know that Period Segmentation can be used, however I would like to have one gross-to-net, which is why I set up Element Segmentation.

✍ ANSWER

System process payroll for the employees until their employment is valid. When the action in the job page is set to 'Termination', the system would automatically reset all employees' accumulators to zero. Whenever the same employee is rehired all his accumulator values would start to resolve and store effective from the date of re-hire.

In that case there could be only two slices in lieu of three as follows:

Slice 1 - Jan 1st to Jan 13th &
Slice 2 - Jan 20th to Jan 31st

The earnings are not calculated for the employee between Jan 14th to Jan 19th.

Should you want to apply different values for the above two slices separately, use recurring page covering the above slices rather than passing as one time input. You cannot have one gross-to-net for the entire process period, as the employee was being terminated and re-hired.

☞ QUESTION 50

Global payroll segmentation issue

I have a problem with segmentation. I have certain elements with a fixed amount that have to be deducted for each payee every month. The problem is when the month is segmented the deduction is done twice.

Example:

Suppose the employee is subject to a deduction of (UNION FEE - Rs.50) and when there is segmentation for the month of July:

    1st segment -1st July to 10th July
    2nd segment -11th July to 31 July

The system deducts 50 Rs. in both the segments resulting in a total deduction of 100 Rs. when it should have been Rs.50 only.

I have tried to prorate the amount but it does not work.

What should I do to resolve this?

✍ ANSWER

You can try setting up a generation control so that the element will resolve in the 1st Active Segment or the last Active Segment. There are some PeopleSoft delivered Generation Controls that do this. This way the entire amount is deducted in one segment only.

☞ QUESTION 51

Emergency_cnct as comp and page

I have a query regarding a PeopleSoft delivered page in self-service called Emergency_cntct as comp and page.

I was given a requirement of maintaining the history data, so I added effdt, effseq fields which PeopleSoft delivered to the record (emergency_cntct) both as keys. However, it is not accepting the data. Its indicating that: "the data you are trying to change does not exist in database".

This error is coming in for some records, but not for all. Is it because of the record I altered which shows they already exist so they do not read as a row? If I build that record separately would it work?

What are my best options to resolve this issue?

✍ ANSWER

It wasn't clear whether you built the record after adding the new fields or not. If not, you do need to build the record. Since this is the way PS communicates with the database with any changes to the structure, unless it's Derived/Work table.

I am presuming these columns which you added are Key columns. If so, try populating them with valid values through the backend for existing rows.

An alternative would be to take the back up of the data and alter the record and build it. Then enter the data again. You may use 'file layout' to enter data.

☞ QUESTION 52

Terminations

If an EE is terminated from JOB_DATA component, does this action add a new row in Health Benefit tables? How do I find out if this is the case?

If an EE is terminated, does this insert a row in BAS Activity?

✍ ANSWER

There are two fields in the Action/Reason table that have to be set up. Ben Status tells the system how to set the employee status when the Action/reason comes through JOB. PeopleBooks will describe each of the statuses for you so you can set them properly. Then there's BAS Action. That tells Ben Admin what to do in the BAS Activity table, as well as the event to process. Setting these values correctly will answer your questions.

For date fields, effective date defaults to today's date when you add the row in JOB. It can be today's date and it can be overridden just like any other effective date field. It should be the date that the change is actually effective, previous or in the future. Except for terms, you have to put in the next day's date. Activity date is the date the transaction was actually processed. It's very helpful when you're trying to decipher what happened when and where you have to insert rows between rows.

☞ QUESTION 53

List of Tables

Where can I find the list of tables related to Base Benefits, Ben Admin, and HR?

✍ ANSWER

Table Loading Sequences can be found on Customer Connection.

Alternatively, you can query a certain table within your PS database and not only get the record names, but also the field names.

☞ QUESTION 54

Canceling GP Processing

Is it possible to cancel the GP Processing in the process monitor page?

Is it possible to cancel and re-run again? Is there any impact by doing so?

✍ ANSWER

GP will calculate payee one by one. Even if you cancel the process during process monitoring; some payee may be already calculated and committed in the database. This is based on the checkpoint interval option. You can rerun the GP process again and it will process the remaining payee. However, it is not advisable to cancel the GP process in process monitor.s

☞ QUESTION 55

Child tables for job, personal data, and employment

I am working on the re-implementation of 8.9 from 7.0 HRMS. While planning the data conversion strategy I found it difficult to know how many tables Job, personal_data, and employment have been normalized in 8.9 from 7.0.

If JOB is a single record in 7.0, it will be split into 4-5 other child records, keeping in mind the normalization changes which occur from 7.0 to 8.9.

What method should I use to get it?

✍ ANSWER

One of the challenges in a reimplementation as opposed to an upgrade is the very situation you are having now. The table structure is just one of the huge changes from 7.0. Throw in navigation and functions that actually work and you have a bigger challenge than just table structures! Hopefully your users will get lots of training!

As for your original question, when upgrading from 7.5 to 8.8, take a "blended" approach. Re-implement in terms of tables and how they were used. The added functionality and the actual technical piece was an upgrade, with custom scripts at the end to handle the customizations to delivered tables. That way you wouldn't miss any child records. It will take 24 hours to convert everything but in the end it will be worth it.

I don't know if there's an upgrade path direct from 7 to 8.9 so you may have to "go through" the 7.5 and 8.8 versions to get there. The table loading sequence document on connection should also be of great help.

You can also get the Data Models from the Customer Connection for the Latest Version. Customer Connection provides 8.0 data models, the JOB table, or what ever table you are using, is normalized into several tables in the latest version. It is better to log a case in customer connection for the latest 8.9 data models, as this will help you on this issue.

☞ QUESTION 56

EMPL_RCD

What is the significance of EMPL_RCD in PS HCM?

Does it represent the number of jobs the employee is currently handling?

✍ ANSWER

Yes, multiple employee records are used for employees having multiple jobs. For example: employees who work in nutrition services as well as grounds maintenance. They have different jobs, positions, and rates of pay.

EMPL_RCD is also used in HCM 8.9 for people with multiple ORG TYPES (Employee vs. Contingent Worker, etc.).

☞ QUESTION 57

Social Security

What is the tax code for Medicare and Social Security in PS and where is it setup?

✍ ANSWER

There is the national ID for payroll, identification & benefits purposes for an individual. In the US they track with a Social Security number. You'll add this data in Workforce Admin > Personal Info >Add. You set this data in Set up HRMS > Foundation Tables>Personal >National ID type.

The tax code for Medicare can be checked in Setup HRMS > Tables>Organization.

☞ QUESTION 58

Global Payroll developers

I'm a recruiter looking for Senior Consultants for Global Payroll and I am having a hard time trying to find a qualified candidate.

We are looking for someone who has 5 years experience with Global Payroll development and 2 implementations. This is a full time position with Bearing Point and I'm simply trying to find candidates but even other recruiters can't help me. Why is this?

✍ ANSWER

Unless you recruit the first people that started the development of Global Payroll you will not find anyone with five years experience in it. This is a hard job since most people that know GP are currently working at a company or assigned to one.

Being a recruiter for Bearing Point you might be able to present an attractive offer. I suggest you add in your note where this position will be located (or alternate options), in which countries it will focus on, what is the pay scale, etc. These factors would definitely attract a few potential candidates.

☞ QUESTION 59

BanAdmin 8.3 Question

We are implementing Benefit Administration 8.3 and I have a question regarding Event Rules.

For the Coverage Begin options, there is an option for Wait Period Days and Wait Period Months. We require a one month waiting period, but does one month convert to 30 days. or does 1 month just go from 6/17 to 7/17, regardless of the number of days? It seems that would be the logical answer, but what happens when the date is 1/31? Does the waiting period end on 2/31, which doesn't exist?

Basically, we want the waiting period to be one month, and then the coverage should begin on the first of the month following 30 days.

How do we accomplish this?

✍ ANSWER

They may not always work out exactly the way you want, but here is how it works:

It begins with the Event Date; then it adds the number of months you specified.
Afterwards, it adds the number of days you specified and then it applies the date it calculates to the Coverage Begin date.

In your specific requirement details, it sounds like a selection of one month will work for the most part. You wouldn't want to use days as the number of days in the month variation.

☞ QUESTION 60

Table Loading Sequence

Where can I find Table Loading Sequence document for eBenefits?

Where can I get into Enterprise component? How about customer connection?

✍ ANSWER

Log into PeopleSoft, then open the application, and then navigate.

Get into Enterprise Components -> Manage Implementations ->Manage Configuration Set and choose the Module for which you want get the data loading document. Your requirement will be generated automatically.

When you get in to Manage Configuration Set, it will ask you to create a configuration set by products & features/process & features. You click configuration set by Product & Features and it will list out the product name. You choose E benefits and view Summary. Then Save. While saving, it will ask you to give the configuration set & Description. Type the product name in both the columns and save.

Then you click 'Generate Set up Tasks'. Refresh, and once the status is changed to posted, Click View Set up Task. You'll get the table loading Documents. Note that it will give you documents for Set UP and not for Transaction.

☞ QUESTION 61

ORIG_HIRE_DT and HIRE_DT

What is the difference between ORIG_HIRE_DT and HIRE_DT? What do these dates represent?

✍ ANSWER

These two dates are used depending on your company policy. Hire date is always used when you are hired or every time you are rehired. Therefore a hire date can be the same as rehire date, if rehired. It can also be the same as ORIG_HIRE_DT. ORIG_HIRE_DT in some companies, is mostly used to calculate benefit related functions such as service years. Again, this depends on your company policy.

An example where both dates are used, is when an employee is terminated and after and later rehired. At the time of re-hire, the HIRE DT changes to the date in which the employee is rehired. In this case, PS has provided these dates so that the employee can retain the benefits from the time when he was originally hired.

☞ QUESTION 62

Action / Reason Global Payroll links

What is a method (even under AD or query) in which Action, Reason or Action/Reason is linked to global payroll process?

I am referring to the 8.8 version.

✍ ANSWER

PeopleSoft doesn't provide any link between Action and Action/Reason combination to Global Payroll. However such a link is available for North American payroll and payroll interface modules. Go through PeopleBooks administer workforce for more information.

You can link the Action/Reason to global payroll elements using generation control pages in set up>product related>global payroll>elements>supporting   elements>generation control>conditions.

You can also link them on Trigger related pages.

If you use MEXICO country extension to Global Payroll you will find several relationships made between ACTION/ REASON and some payroll procedures, as they relate to IMSS (Social Security).

The information for this can be seen in the fields:

IMS_TER_REASON_MEX
INF_REASON_MEX
SUA_REASON_MEX
IMS_PRN_FORM_MEX
MAINT_VAR_SDI_MEX

To see what these fields mean you can run:

SELECT * FROM PSXLATITEM
WHERE FIELDNAME IN ('IMS_TER_REASON_MEX', 'INF_
REASON_MEX', 'SUA_REASON_MEX', 'IMS_PRN_FORM_
MEX', 'MAINT_VAR_SDI_MEX')

Action determines the employee status. Only status is set to Active, Leave with Pay, Retired with Pay, or Terminated with Pay, PS will trigger Global Payroll processing.

☞ QUESTION 63

Global Payroll – Identify

On what basis does the payroll processing Cobol SQR identify the employees for payroll computations?

We have configured a system where we have 3 pay entities within the same country. The issue I am facing is that an employee who was transferred from one pay entity to another on Nov 04 is continually being identified in his old Pay entity. Since we ran the entire 3 pay entities payroll we got a payee message. We have to cancel the employee's payee status in the old pay entity every month before finalizing.

For transferring we have added a termination record in the old Pay entity and rehired him in the new pay entity.

Is there a better way to do this?

✍ ANSWER

Global Payroll in Mexico has had similar situations. More than the 'Identify' phase, the situation results from the segmentation that occurs due to the changes in JOB DATA.

The Identify process will look at what you have defined in you Calendar (Active Payees or Listed Payees).

Place a 'workaround' to avoid what you are facing. Create a job that looks at active employees for the company, pay group, pay entity, calendar and create a Payee List into each calendar. From there, run the payroll.

There are other solutions which can solve the transfer issue from one Pay Group to another. You can follow one of the alternatives below:

1. Put the 3 Calendars (one Calendar for one Pay Entity) in one Calendar Group.

2. If the 3 Pay Entities are not in the same Calendar Group. Run and finalize them one by one as a payee can not be identified by more than one OPENED Calendar Group. Then this payee will be calculated in each Pay Entity and you can define the prorating rules for them.

Both of the above two solutions have some limitations. Suppose that a payee is transferred from Pay Group A to Pay Group B, or some payroll elements are calculated in the last segment. Try to use the accumulator based on the whole pay period. These elements should be calculated in Calendar B. Another payee maybe transfers from B to A. Which Calendar should be run first, A or B?

3. Another solution is that you can use Payee Calendar Group Override. This is the PS standard function for Global Payroll. You can cancel the identification in one Pay Entity and let the whole pay period be calculated in another Pay Entity. For more details, please refer to the PeopleBooks.

☞ QUESTION **64**

PERS Rate Change during Split Earnings Payroll

We are a Washington State employer, subject to the new PERS (Public Employees Retirement Savings) rate changes effective July 1st, 2005. The first paycheck this will affect is split between June and July earnings. How would you set your system up to use the old rate for June earnings and the new rate for July earnings?

Currently the deduction is set-up in benefits to use a special accumulator to capture all includable earnings within the pay period, but it does not separate each month's earnings.

We are currently using version 8.801 SP1.

✍ ANSWER

The earnings table is effectively dated, so you shouldn't have any problems with this. It isn't much different than changes in pay or earnings at the beginning of a calendar year when the pay period crosses the years.

PeopleSoft HRMS Interview Questions, Answers, and Explanations

☞ QUESTION 65

Job Function & Job Family Issue

I need to clarify some things related to Job Function & Job Family.

Can I have a Job Function as 'HR' and the Job Family as 'Recruitment', 'Learning & Dev', 'Visa Processing' or should it be the other way with HR as Job Family & Job function as Recruitment, etc.?

What are the advantages and disadvantages of each alternative?

Are these flexible to changes?

✍ ANSWER

It should be the other way around. The Family is HR and the function is Recruitment.

Below is a sample of a DEMO database JOB_FUNCITION with the following 19 values:

ADM Administration
AUD Internal Audit
COM Communications
ENG Engineering Services
FIN Finance and Accounting
HRS Human Resources
LEG Legal

- 86 -

LND Lending
MGT Management
MIS Information System
MKT Marketing
MNF Manufacturing
OPS Operations
PLN Planning
PRD Product Engineering
PUR Purchasing
REL Commercial & Industry
RES Research/Development

While JOB_FAMILY only has 5 values:

KADMIN Administrative Support
KCLERK Clerical
KTECH Information Technology
LHUMAN Human Resources
LTECH Technical

There really is not much in JOB_FAMILY to point in one direction or another, I am of the opinion that JOB_FUNCTION points to the 'broader' scope of Function.

There are 7 tables with the field JOB_FUNCTION and 27 views; this field is used in 26 'pages' with no clear area of usage. I know that JOB_FUNCTION has been part of the system since, at least, 1991.

There are 15 tables with the field JOB_FAMILY and 26 views; this field is used in 9 'pages'. It is very obvious that JOB_FAMILY is very close to Competency Management, which entered the application with release 5, 6 or 7.

Job Function and Job Family are two different ways to

categorize jobs. It is entirely your prerogative how you would like to use them. But two things to take into consideration while judging whether it's a Job family or Job Function is:

1. Job Function is used as Job category in Apply for Jobs / job search agent in recruiting self service module. Hence if I want to group jobs to help a candidate for applying for a job area like Finance, HR or some product line I create Job function by that name and assign related jobs like accounting, costing, etc to that Function. We used 14 job functions as Manufacturing, HR, Finance, Marketing, etc.

2. Set up common competencies for group jobs you can define in Job profile. Then attach job profile to Job family. How the group jobs are based on competencies is an organizational prerogative. Here competencies are grouped by domain of work (HR domain knowledge and skills needed by all in HR) and type of role (for manager's role across functions common set of competencies etc). In this organization, HR wants a different group for a combination of domain and role. For example: A job family as HR- Team Member, HR- Manager etc.

☞ QUESTION 66

Non Employee Concept

What is the concept of "Non employee having EMPLID in PS HCM"?

What does "Non Employee" represent in PS HCM?

✍ ANSWER

Non-employees are contractors, trainers, people taking training at your company, members of the board, etc. They can be vendors, too. They're people you aren't paying a salary, but still need to keep track of or use elsewhere in the system, as in training or security.

☞ QUESTION 67

Original hire date vs. hire date

I understand that the original hire date of personal data table is the date on which the employee was hired in the company (or in the group to which this company belongs) for the first time. The hire date of Employment table is the date (effdt) the employee was hired in the PeopleSoft system for the first time. In our system we have a few with hire date older than the original hire date and this is confusing.

What is the difference between original hire date as compared to hire date?

✍ ANSWER

The original rehire date is used if the employee has been rehired. It will maintain the original date of hire for that employees ID, and the hire date is the rehire date.

Check the data mapping whether they are correctly mapped or not.

Your original hire date should be the oldest one on file. It is the date the employee was first hired with the company. It shouldn't be reset by any other action/reason. If you're seeing Hire Dates older than OHD, I'd look at a conversion from a previous system or an acquisition perhaps. and someone did the data mapping wrong.

The only time you should see an original hire date on personal data different than the hire date on employment, is when you are using multiple jobs (empl_rcd <> 0). Otherwise the two are the same. Rehire date is a different field.

In an acquisition, it's not unusual to see on Original Date of Hire (part of the PERSON data table set) reflect the employee's date of hire with the original employer, while the HIR row on JOB reflects the date of hire with the acquiring company. That's not right, and it will cause problems, particularly for the pension module, if you have it, but it does happen at several sites.

The dates can also get out of synch if a user enters hire information for a prospective new hire, and later has to adjust the HIR row to reflect a different date. I'm not certain if there is PC behind the scenes to correct it in the most current release, but historically this has been a problem.

The HIRE DATE on EMPLOYMENT gets populated by the PC on JOB when a HIR row is entered.

☞ QUESTION **68**

Manage Hire Issue in Talent Acquisition Mgr (E Recruit) 8.9

This is a critical issue I am facing in HRMS 8.9. When I recruit a candidate, the details should be reflected in Manage Hires Page in WorkforceAdmin>Personal info>Org Relationships>Manage Hires.

However, it is not reflecting. When the status is set to "Offer Accepted" for a candidate you go for "Prepare for hire". At that time when you click save & request submit to HR, it should be transferred to HR Data Base. I got a workaround for that from Customer Connection. They asked me to add a counter value in a table and I added it. They asked me to add query role. I added Role_Hire_Notif. "Integration Broker" is active but it isn't working.

This is the role query:

```
SELECT B.EMAILID
FROM PSOPRDEFN B, PSROLEUSER A
WHERE EXISTS (SELECT D.HIRE_REQUEST_ID
FROM PS_HR_REQUEST D
WHERE D.HIRE_REQUEST_ID = :1)
AND B.OPRID = A.ROLEUSER
AND A.ROLENAME = 'HR Administrator'
```

We are currently using workflow for routing.

Should I configure something else in Integration Broker or is it related with Query?

✍ ANSWER

If you are using workflow for routing, just go through the role query you added, and check the permission lists also.

Clear any error messages via the Message Monitor. If there's one there, it stops your 'ready for hires' getting through to HR.

☞ QUESTION 69

M&A activities

How do you handle bringing in employees from M&A activity into your PeopleSoft system or into Custom SQRs, Application Engine programs, and other such departments?

Q2: What I am more curious about is the technical solutions people have tried, not so much the business requirements. In the past I have used SQRs to import the new company data. More recently I have started using App Engine / CI. This took considerably more time (to run that is; development was significantly quicker), but are defect rate was down near zero. Are there any Peoplesoft or third party tools to help with M&A activities?

✍ ANSWER

Mergers & Acquisitions are always challenging. First and foremost, do an exceptional job with the source data analysis and mapping. Dates and history are critical later on. Next, create HIR row for your first row, not a Data Conversion row. If you must, and you probably will, create dummy jobs, locations, and departments. Look at your source system and get the earliest date you can for your HIR row. Then you create the data conversion row, effective with the date of the acquisition and all your new data structures.

As for getting the data in, use custom SQR's more often. They are easier to create and test, and you can order them correctly.

During your initial data conversion you must create two rows in PS_JOB.

The first should have an ACTION of HIR, and the EFFDT should be the Actual Hire Date of the employee, NOT the 'conversion' date.

The second should have an ACTION of CNV, and the EFFDT should be the Date of Conversion.

Everything else on these two rows can be exactly the same.

Another alternative would be the Application Engine: CI architecture. Usually by the time you are halfway through coding the data conversion process, the customization team has added three new fields and reams of PeopleCode logic to the target records. By using the CI you can let the component processor handle these changes, rather than doing a find replace on all "INSERT INTO PS_JOB" instances in your SQR folder.

I would also recommend that you do all data conversion within the PeopleSoft architecture. You can create a raft of staging tables that handle the old to new mapping within the PeopleSoft instance. This way you can validate your mapping tables much more readily than if they are sitting on a spreadsheet on somebody's c:\ drive.

For example, the current data migration goes something like:

1) Load source data into source staging tables (the look and feel should be as close to the old system as possible).

2) Build Data Entry tables based on these source staging tables (rather than building a clone of job, just build a

record that contains the fields you need to enter data into the HIRE component).

3) Loop through the Data Entry tables, for each row trigger a CI passing in the relevant data.

4) Handle and record any messages generated by the CI tagging the corresponding row in the Data Entry table.

By keeping everything within the PS database, you can cross reference all the exceptions and track them. Instead of wading through 20+ SQR.LOG files, you have a simple query page that allows you to track messages by employee, by process, by message severity etc.

In this way you can effectively audit each datum that is sent to you, either proving that it was successfully entered into the system or that it was rejected and why.

☞ QUESTION **70**

HR Tables Content Question

In HR 8.8, what tables would I find "FUND" besides ACCT_CD_TBL?

How do I link employee with DEPTID and FUND?

✍ ANSWER

Always use account code. What's stored in it, or what it's called, is up to your GL or Budget system. As a matter of fact, you should encourage all clients to have the GL system send the Account Code Table to PS and have it set as view only.

You can run this query:

"SELECT * FROM PSRECFIELD WHERE FIELDNAME = 'FUND_CODE'"

In a regular database, there are 24 tables with this field.

☞ QUESTION 71

Add a new translate value to a field

How can we add a new translate value to a field in 8.45/8.8 if the field already exists?

✍ ANSWER

In field properties, translate values tab; add new values using add translate values, and you can do editing, deleting or de-activate them.

You can also do this online, through PeopleTools --> Utilities --> Administration --> Translate Values.

Then search for the appropriate field name, insert a row, and save.

Take note though, that if you want to migrate them between environments, then use application designer, and add them to a project.

Apart from adding the translate values in Application Designer & PeopleTools>Utilities>Admin>Translate Tables, you can also add translate values for the Personal & JOb DAta Page of your WorkForce Admin in PeopleTools>Foun dationTables.

☞ QUESTION 72

Recruitment Issue Related to Business Unit

There are some bugs in Talent Acquisition Manager via E Recruit which blocks me from rolling out my Recruitment Module.

When I create a Job Opening with Business Unit GBIBU from PS User Login, I can see the Job Opening in careers link. When I create a Job Opening from my own Business Unit, I couldn't see the Job Created in Careers Link.

I have a Single Business Unit. I have set the related Set IDs and Control Ids.

How do I trace the problem and resolve it?

✍ ANSWER

You need to create a Site ID with which to link the Business Unit, Site ID & Permission list. Unless you create a Site ID for your Business Unit, the Job Opening will not reflect in Careers.

☞ QUESTION 73

Mid-year Pay-period change from Semi-monthly to Bi-weekly

How do I effectively change pay cycles mid-year from monthly to bi-weekly?

What are the effects on Payroll as well as Time & Labor?

What issues should I anticipate?

✍ ANSWER

One thing you will want to consider is your deduction frequencies and amounts. If you are calculating pay period amounts you may need to recalculate the amounts of your deductions and benefit deductions.

One of the issues that come up when changing pay frequency is a perceived "shortfall", especially if you implement a lag pay in there. Goal balances are an issue. Leave accruals may be also, depending on how you accrue.

☞ QUESTION 74

Maintain Contractors/Temp Employees in HCM88 SP1

How do I maintain Contractor/Temp Employees details in HCM88?

✍ ANSWER

To add contractors to your database, choose Workforce Admin>Increase Workforce>Add Non-employees. This will allow you to store all the information for them, as you do for employees. You will add them, not hire them. On their Job Information page, select an Employee Class of Contractor.

As far as the temporary employees are concerned, it will depend on what kind of temporary employees they are. Are they your employee or are they from an agency? If the former, you need to add them to you database just like any other employee. You can change their Regular/Temporary field to Temporary. If the latter, then you can add them as Non-employees, change their Regular/Temporary field to Temporary and select an Employee Class of Agency/ Temporary.

Depending on how you pay them, i.e., payroll or AP, there can be other considerations, but I think the above will get you started. The Administer Workforce PeopleBooks also has information on this topic.

☞ QUESTION 75

PeopleSoft or SAP-HRMS

I am looking to enter the HRMS field, but unable to reach any consensus due to the uncertainty of the PeopleSoft HRMS module.

I'm on the threshold of a new career and a wrong move would spell disaster.

Which is better to learn, PeopleSoft HRMS or SAP HRMS?

✍ ANSWER

In my opinion PeopleSoft is head and shoulders above the other two.

At most, Oracle will rename the product and call it something else, but it wouldn't make sense for anyone to do away with the leading product on the market, especially since they own it!

☞ QUESTION 76

Electronic Pay Stubs

We are looking to outsource our electronic pay stubs. We initially looked at ePay from PeopleSoft, however the cost was high for a small company. (I think it was $44,000 when PeopleSoft was PeopleSoft, now its $64,000 with Oracle.)

What company is recommended that outsource their pay stubs? If so, would you recommend the company?

✍ ANSWER

You might try TALX.

You might try this, also. www.workforce.com. There is a section called Vendor Directory. They have lots of links and comparisons for vendors of all types. You can also go to the Topic Forums and put a posting under the Technology and HR Systems section and ask others their opinions. You do have to register but it's free.

☞ QUESTION 77

Archive PSAUDIT

Our PSAUDIT table contains 8.3 million lines and our DBA suggests creating a PSAUDIT archive table to store audit data prior to 2005.

Has this been done before? What would be the consequences?

✍ ANSWER

You just need to make sure that any processes which interrogate PSAUDIT, look at a view which UNIONS your PSAUDIT and PSAUDIT_ARCHIVE records.

If you are auditing several fields on a record, you might want to consider switching to record level auditing rather than using PSAUDIT. Field level is great for one or two fields, but if you are tracing several fields it becomes a nightmare trying to reconstruct the value of a row at any given time.

☞ QUESTION 78

Global Payroll performance

We are seeing a drop in performance for a Global Payroll of some 4,000 employees (SQLServer 2000, NT2000 GP8.8 PT8.44).

On Jan 4th it took 2.5 hours, on Jan 9 it took 4 hours.

Our DBA people are looking into it, our internal PSFT team is at a loss since this is new to them. I am at a loss too, being functional and, seeing this drop in performance for the first time.

I have looked into Customer Connection and am forwarding some documents to our DBA people hoping they can be of help.

What could be the cause of the problem here? How do we resolve this issue?

✍ ANSWER

Here is my favorite tip:

I have seen sudden slow downs due to a new rule being created causing a huge amount of unnecessary element processing. I see this with companies processing 40,000-200,000 payees.

What you can do is to enable batch timings via psprcs.cfg, or in the Override Options in Process Definition. Also add a comment in the stored statements e.g. DELETE /*GPPCANCL_

D_CANWRK*/FROM PS_GP_CANCEL_WRK WHERE EMPLID
BETWEEN: 1 AND:
2 AND CAL_RUN_ID=:3
Sample output:

PeopleSoft Batch Statistics:

Encoding Scheme Used: Ansi

Retrieve Compile Execute Fetch STMT TOTALS
Statement Count Time Count Time Count Time Count Time
Time % SQL

(Unknown) 0 0.00 0 0.00 2445 49.54 0 0.00 49.54 -0.12
COMMIT 0 0.00 0 0.00 70 6.00 0 0.00 6.00 -0.01
CONNECT 0 0.00 0 0.00 159 1.20 0 0.00 1.20 -0.00
DISCONNECT 0 0.00 0 0.00 159 0.07 0 0.00 0.07 -0.00
DYNAMIC 0 0.00 2 0.00 19 14.73 377 0.02 14.75 -0.04
GPPCANCL_D_AUDIT 1 0.01 1 0.00 1 0.00 0 0.00 0.01 -0.00
GPPCANCL_D_CANWRK 2 0.01 2 0.00 2 0.00 0 0.00 0.01 -0.00
GPPCANCL_D_FAUDIT 1 0.01 1 0.00 1 0.00 0 0.00 0.01 -0.00
GPPCANCL_D_FICTPRC 1 0.00 1 0.00 1 0.71 0 0.00 0.71 -0.00
GPPCANCL_D_FICTSEG 1 0.00 1 0.00 1 0.77 0 0.00 0.77 -0.00
GPPCANCL_D_FMSGSC 1 0.00 1 0.00 1 0.01 0 0.00 0.01 -0.00
GPPCANCL_D_MSGSC 1 0.01 1 0.00 1 0.34 0 0.00 0.35 -0.00
GPPCANCL_D_MSGSI 1 0.01 1 0.00 1 0.00 0 0.00 0.01 -0.00
GPPCANCL_D_PIDATA 1 0.00 1 0.00 1 44.45 0 0.00 44.45 -0.11
GPPCANCL_D_PIHDRC 1 0.01 1 0.00 1 2.80 0 0.00 2.81 -0.01
GPPCANCL_D_PIHDRR 1 0.01 1 0.00 1 0.14 0 0.00 0.15 -0.00
GPPCANCL_D_PIREF 1 0.01 1 0.00 1 7.71 0 0.00 7.72 -0.02
GPPCANCL_D_PISOVR 1 0.00 1 0.00 1 80.87 0 0.00 80.87 -0.20
GPPCANCL_D_PRC 1 0.00 1 0.00 1 1.40 0 0.00 1.40 -0.00
GPPCANCL_D_RDELTA 1 0.00 1 0.01 1 2.23 0 0.00 2.24 -0.01
GPPCANCL_D_RSLTABS 1 0.00 1 0.00 1 8.90 0 0.00 8.90 -0.02
GPPCANCL_D_RSLTACM 1 0.01 1 0.00 1 133.34 0 0.00 133.35

-0.33

GPPCANCL_D_RSLTERN 1 0.00 1 0.00 1 10.25 0 0.00 10.25 - 0.03

GPPCANCL_D_RSLTPID 1 0.00 1 0.00 1 16.02 0 0.00 16.02 - 0.04

GPPCANCL_D_RSLTPIN 1 0.00 1 0.00 1 108.36 0 0.00 108.36 -0.26

GPPCANCL_D_RSLTPIS 1 0.01 1 0.00 1 9.35 0 0.00 9.36 -0.02

GPPCANCL_D_RSLTSEG 1 0.00 1 0.01 1 2.18 0 0.00 2.19 -0.01

GPPCANCL_D_SEG 1 0.00 1 0.00 1 3.03 0 0.00 3.03 -0.01

GPPCANCL_I_CANWRK 1 0.03 1 0.00 1 2.37 0 0.00 2.40 -0.01

You can then identify which SQL statements to target.

Retro is another thing you might like to investigate. There was an instance after data migration where employees had triggers created that were before the retro limits for their pay group. That meant that during each pay run the pay system was dragging in every prior calendar in an attempt to get back to the trigger. However, because it hit the retro limit before it hit the trigger, it could never clear out the trigger. This gives you a geometric increase in run times. At the beginning this wasn't too bad, but after three pay cycles they were bringing in 3 pay calendars worth of retro. After running 30 pay cycles, you bring in 30 historic calendars of data for the affected employee(s). This can seriously impacts performance.

Retro Limits are also appropriate. If your have the CPU, you could consider using Streaming with Partitioned Tables, and if you're already doing that, rebalancing your streams from time to time will help.

☞ QUESTION 79

Approvals in Talent Acquisition Manager 8.9

I had set the values for Approvals in SetUpHRMS>CommonD efinition>Approvals for both Job Opening and Job Approval. When I create Job Opening and Submit Save & Open, instead of showing the Approvals Page it shows me "No Approvals Required".

What should I do to activate the approvals?

✎ ANSWER

Make sure you check boxes on the Recruitment Installation table. Then set up HRMS>Install>Product and Country Specific>Recruiting Installation.

To make it simpler you can have all the User lists as role and attach to user id in Security.

☞ QUESTION 80

Bug in Talent Acquisition Manager 8.9

When you a hire a Person, in the final step in eRecruit the details of the Applicant are not forwarded to HR Database.

Did PeopleSoft provide a MP or can we go for a workaround?

✍ ANSWER

This is not a bug, but a missing configuration that should be there. Check out PeopleTools > Integration Broker > Gateways. The Local Gateway needs to be set up correctly or Recruitment will not talk to HR.

☞ QUESTION 81

eRecruit v8.9

Is there an online link to PeopleBook v8.9 for public use?

My company is going to implement eRecruit v8.9 and we are currently in the process to prepare the blueprint.

How do we implement this?

✍ ANSWER

There is no legal public link for this material.

If your company is implementing it soon, then someone in your company has a link to Customer Connection. They can order PeopleBooks for you. There is no legal way to buy, sell or receive topics of PeopleBooks outside of Customer Connection.

☞ **QUESTION 82**

How to debug COBOL program

How can we debug a COBOL program online in PeopleSoft?

✍ **ANSWER**

It is almost impossible to perform an online COBOL debug. You can however run a SQL trace to follow the SQL activity and derive the COBOL code from that.

If you have access to some of the more advanced COBOL compiler tools, you can run an online step through your code using the compiler harness, but this is not for the faint of heart.

Sometimes turning on the resolution chain can help you track how a particular element is resolving itself in GP if that is what you are trying to trace.

Failing that, you need to get the source files, add in some debug statements, and then re-compile.

☞ QUESTION 83

Improve processing times of HR

I am being tasked to take on PeopleSoft HRMS "processing times" performance tuning.

I am familiar with the concurrent manager on oracle financials 11i, and the whole tech stack. I have worked with PeopleSoft before, but it's been a while.
What would be the first thing to look at as far as the Application in the Tuxedo layer or the Process Scheduler? Is there anyway to tune that?

Here are some more details.

I use commands like iostat,sar,top,vmstat to look at the actual server to identify if there is a bottleneck on the server to determine if the problem is in the CPU, I/O or memory.

Take the web server and the application server. I've read in technical documents that the application server is where most shops struggle with appropriate sizing.

Is this true or is this a fallacy?

✍ ANSWER

Tuning your Application Server can provide some really good gains in performance, but it is not always the bottle neck.

Depending on your tools version, the BBL can start quite a

few different services. The generic workhorse PSAPPSRV is a jack of all trades that can do just about anything. Some of the other services are quite task specific. PeopleBooks and you PSAPPSRV.CFG file contain some ideas about what the other services do and when it is a good idea to start them.

In general the first thing you should do is get a CPU usage history together for each of the tiers in your PIA. This will give you an idea as to where the bottle necks are.

Assuming that your web server and data base do not max out their CPU usage, then your Application Server may be the bottleneck.

For example, on one site where we there was poor performance, the CPU usage averaged 20-30% during peak periods. Inspection of the BBL showed that there were only 3 PSAPPSRV processes running, and they were running non-stop, there was no idle time. Obviously on a production type environment, 3 instances of PSAPPSRV are ridiculously underpowered. CPU and RAM both showed plenty of spare capacity, and so increasing PSAPPSRV instances provided significant performance gains.

Tuning the Process Scheduler is less of a science. Essentially as long as your sleep time isn't too low for the scheduler and the distribution agent, the work is half done. Having too much tracing / logging going on, can also slow you down.

☞ QUESTION 84

Conversion: Employee Data Loading Sequence

Does anyone have a conversion table loading sequence for employee data?

✍ ANSWER

If by EMPLOYEE you mean data related to the 'employees' in the organization you can start by doing the following:

1. Navigate to the panels that have the data you need. For example: Workforce Administration > Personal Information > Biographical > Update Personal Information.

   Once there, press CTRL-J and you will see some information. Copy the text nex to "Page".

2. Run SELECT DISTINCT(FIELDNAME), RECNAME FROM PSPNLFIELD WHERE PNLNAME = 'PERSONAL_DATA1' ORDER BY 2,1;

[[replace the text "PERSONAL_DATA1" with the name of each page you are looking for.]]
The result will list each and every field with its corresponding table, that is used in each page.

You will have to disregard some tables like those titled "DERIVEDxxx" and those from other countries, etc.

☞ QUESTION 85

Question on use of Ben Status field

What is the BEN_STATUS field on the action reason table used for?

If the value is 'A', does it imply that a payroll action might be associated with it?

✍ ANSWER

As far as JOB DATA is concerned (and Payroll as a result) the status of an employee (EMPL_STATUS) is determined by the ACTION. The valid values for this field are:

A Active
D Deceased
L Leave of Absence
P Leave With Pay
Q Retired With Pay
R Retired
S Suspended
T Terminated
U Terminated With Pay
V Terminated Pension Pay Out
W Short Work Break
X Retired-Pension Administration

But when you look at Benefits, things can be different. You can terminate a person for payroll but still provide benefits. As a result the field you refer too takes care of setting the

BEN_STATUS for the employee.

The valid values for this field are:
  A Active
  D Deceased
  L Leave of Absence
  P Leave with Benefits
  Q Retired with Benefits
  R Retired
  S Suspended
  T Terminated
  U Terminated With Benefits

So, for example:

If you assign ACTION="TER" the system will set - - - EMPL_ STATUS="T" and BEN_STATUS="T"
if you assign ACTION="TWB" the system will set - - EMPL_ STATUS="T" and BEN_STATUS="U";

☞ QUESTION 86

Import data in a Row into a Pre-Populated Word Template

I am trying to figure if it is possible to export data from a Row in PeopleSoft into a Word Template for printing purposes. My guess is that if we could take data from a Grid and export to Excel. or Run a query to Excel, we should be able to do the same with Microsoft Word.

Is this possible?

✍ ANSWER

You may want to look at the delivered letters in the Standard Letter table. There are instructions in PeopleBooks about adding letters and the SQR that populates them.

All you have to do is: create SQR that populates a flat file/data file with the row of data. Create a WinWord process with append parameters looking at the STDLTR.doc templates (or any other docs that are based on this template).

Write a macro specifying the location of the template, location of the data files, and the output location. You can look at any of the existing SQR's. app004.SQR is a great example.

☞ QUESTION 87

Imputed income configuration with vendors

We are currently outsourcing our life insurance plans to a vendor who will not calculate imputed income for us. We need to calculate these ourselves, but the vendor will be maintaining the life plans on their systems. Our best guess is to take enrollment information for the life plans and age-graded rate tables from the vendor, feed these into the Life ADD tables, and let PS calculate the imputed income as normal. The actual employee deduction amounts that the vendor calculates and sends to us, we are planning to dump into general deductions in payroll.

Will this get the job done?

Is there a workaround for this issue?

✍ ANSWER

I am not sure why you would need a third party if you're going to have to emulate the entire process, but that's up to you. Yes, the process you've described will result in the calculation of the life insurance volume. However, imputed income calculates based on plan type 20; it is not a general deduction.

☞ QUESTION 88

Deadlock victim

As we where running payroll (GP 8.8 with Mexico extension) we had the following error:

"Transaction (Process ID 66) was deadlocked on lock resources with another process and has been chosen as the deadlock victim".

We had a payroll process for one company (about 4500 employees) running at the same time as a second payroll process for another company (about 3500 employees). Each company has its own Calendars and Calendar Group. They share most of the elements. We chose to run them separately since they are assigned to different people in the organization.

As I understand it, the error was created because both processes are trying to access the same table. What I do not understand is how companies with much larger populations can handle their volume and distributed organizations.

How can I best handle this issue?

✍ ANSWER

The solution for this it to add a field to where the clause of the SQL statement in question is causing row locking instead of table locking. Unfortunately this happens in temporary tables more often than anyone would like to admit, like locking the entire table when it was only intended to lock specific rows.

☞ QUESTION 89

Rate Code/ Step Pay

We're currently on 8.3.

We want to use rate codes for additional pay. like stipends for example, and attach them to the job code. We also use step pay. As delivered, it appears that if you use steps, you have to associate the rate code with the step not the job. This sounds silly, because I can have people in different jobs, but use the same salary grade and step. I don't want to customize, but it looks like we may have to.

My developer thinks all we need to do is comment out an "IF" statement.

How do I fix this issue in the most expedient manner?

✍ ANSWER

I would encourage you to take a look at the release notes for version 8.9 and the new Wage Progression functionality that is delivered in this newest version. There is a complete overhaul of the functionality here that I believe will solve your problem. By the way, if you are currently on 8.3, you will need to begin looking at an upgrade, as the support for that version will expire in the near future.

☞ QUESTION 90

Compensation Rate

I'm a beginner user of PeopleSoft. I am working in the implementation for my company.

When I run a query with the comp_rate, it shows in the right format, e.g.18000.00. But when I download the query to an Excel file it appears wrong: 18.000.000.000.

What can I do to reach the right format in Excel?

✍ ANSWER

It seems something is wrong here. In HR & Global Payroll 8.8, there is no such thing as "comp_rate", there is only COMPRATE.

On you other question:

"I get results like...
000001 75870.000000
000002 29590.000000"

This should work ok when moved to Excel.

☞ **QUESTION 91**

PS_PERSONAL_DATA and PS_JOB

I've just started to study PeopleSoft tables in order to extract some data for a data warehouse.

I have some doubt about the tables PS_JOB and PS_PERSONAL_ DATA. These tables seem important but, with application designer, I've never seen a PeopleSoft page. There is not a field in these pages that interact with these two tables.

I noticed that PS directly works with these tables: PS_NAMES, PS_ADDRESSES, PS_FPAEECAREER and others.

This is what I assumed:

That PS works directly with tables (PS_NAMES, PS_ ADDRESSES, and PS_FPAEECAREER), which contains all the history data. Some batches are launched in order to aggregate this data into PS_JOB and PS_PERSONAL_DATA, which ONLY contains the last situation (the history is handle by S_NAMES, PS_ADDRESSES, PS_FPAEECAREER;

Is my assumption correct?

✍ **ANSWER**

You should have three basic data groups:

Personal Data (a name, an address, a sex, a birth date, etc.);
Employment data (a hire date, a service date, etc.);

JOB data (a location, a position, a compensation rate, etc.);

Back in the old days Personal Data had ALL the information about the person. Since it has all been split into several tables and, as has been pointed, the PERSON model on 8.9 will put an end to this table. This table was not EFFDTed back then, and has also evolved. This table assigns the EMPLID.

EMPLOYMENT is a child of PERSONAL DATA and is the one that assigns the EMPL_RCD.

JOB is a child of EMPLOYMENT and since it tracks all your moves in the company it will, through time, have several rows per employee. This table assigns EFFDT and EFFSEQ.

And these four fields are your keys to a lot of other places.

☞ QUESTION 92

Benefits Reconciliation

How do other companies reconcile employee benefit deductions?

Currently I ran a query of all active employees and if they elected benefits. Then I run another query to see how much was deducted (at the end of the month). Then I visually compare the two reports for discrepancies. This is very time consuming and I know there must be a better way.

Does PeopleSoft have a similar report or suggestion on how to create a custom query or SQL to accomplish this task?

✍ ANSWER

There are delivered registers that show what was deducted for each employee as well as a separate register that shows what wasn't deducted. You can always create a custom one if the delivered ones don't work for you, but most people manage to use the delivered ones just fine.

☞ QUESTION **93**

e-Development Training Administrator

We are looking into implementing e-Development for Training and Manager self-service training enrollment. When setting everything up, there is a Training Administrator role. It seems that this role is used for all transactions in all locations.

My concern is, Manager A approves emplid B's training request. It is then forwarded to the training administrator to approve and update the database. If we have one training administrator at each location, I would like them only to see and be able to approve the requests from their location. Currently, it is delivered in such a manner that all training administrators can see and approve all requests.

We are on HRMS 8.8 sp1 and up to date on all bundles.

How can I configure it such that the training administrator can only administer requests from his/her location?

✍ ANSWER

You see all of the users with that role associated with their user id because the delivered role is 'static' meaning it goes to all. You need to modify the role or create your own custom role and integrate it into the workflow so that it is a role 'Query'. This will route the workflow to the appropriate user id based on the selection criteria of the query.

☞ QUESTION 94

Implementation and Customization Projects

I have some questions:

1. What is an implementation and customization project? What are their differences?
2. In an implementation project, I set all tables and calculations. What about SQR reports?
3. Is version PS HR8.8/8.4 used in the US? If so when is it being used?
4. What is e-pay and e-benefit? Are these available in 8.x versions and not in 7.5?

✍ ANSWER

PS 8.8 came into being first quarter 2003. The major differences are that it's all on the web, nothing on the client, and the navigation is very different than any prior release. It is much more intuitive.

A lot of companies use a different terminology for their "implementation" projects. At a basic level, you "implement" the package in its vanilla form in the way it comes out of the box, so to speak. Customizations are done when the delivered product won't meet all your needs, which you should have discovered and documented in a FIT/GAP phase. The "Gaps" are where a customization would be done although I suggest that you change a business process where you can, rather than changing the package.

The "e' modules (e-Pay, e-Ben, etc.) are the internet applications for employees to perform their own tasks, such as setting up their own direct deposit, enroll for benefits or change their address/phone/emergency contact, etc. They eliminate paper, are more timely and accessible, and the employee knows all the information, so let them change it.

Meanwhile, implementation is the act of taking the product out of the box, configuring the needed tables, defining the needed values and loading the needed data. All of these things are done without making any changes to records, fields, menus, pages, peoplecode, etc.

Customization is the act of adding, modifying or deleting application objects (records, fields, menus, pages, peoplecode, etc.).

We all try a hard as we can to stay more on the 'implementation' side than on the 'customization' side.

Reports are very much a part of your implementation. Many times reports are assigned low priority and tend to fall between the cracks. If this happens you will have a huge problem once you go live. There is more impact in Payroll than in HR. Try to avoid this as much as you can.

Similarly we can say the same about interfaces to/from other systems.

All PSFT products are basically 'global' and are in use everywhere especially in the US where PSFT easily leads the marketplace in terms of users. There are several places on PSFT applications where functionality unique to one country is added. The US is no exception to this (FLSA, HIIPA, etc.).

The "e" modules are only available from 8x on. They are also called 'collaborative applications'. They are characterized by the fact that they are used by employees and managers outside of those on the specific function. For example: the company has a 'benefits' department that uses the "BENEFITS" applications. With 'eBenefits' employees can see their own coverage, elections and options. If existing, there will be links to the benefits providers (BP) so that PSFT 'collaborates' with the BP application in providing service and information to employees.

☞ QUESTION 95

Benefits

I have a couple of questions.

1. The client is interested in giving a new benefit that is not in PeopleSoft like some yearly cash plan(retirement) which says for 0-4 yrs of service you will be given 5% of your gross pay(annual payment), for 6-10yrs - 10%. I don't have this in PeopleSoft. This benefit is purely company specific.

Yearly Cash Plan (Retirement) Details:

Basis of Computation: Years of service % credit on GP: Indicators

　0-4 yrs 5%
　5-10 yrs 7%
　11-15 yrs 9%
　Above 15 12%

How do I configure this?

2. What are the customizations possible in benefits administration and payroll? What are the customizations possible in reports in both?

✍ Answer

This is about retirement benefits which is solely a company specific policy. Since PeopleSoft does not work on this type of functionality, you can simply create an age rated table like the one you mentioned. You create an SQR using the service dates/hire dates of employees and get the percentage from the table then use this percentage to get the desired amounts. The question is when you run this functionality. Here's some simple step to carry out your function.

1. Create the age rated table.
2. Create online screen to maintain the table.
3. Create SQR to produce a report and earnings file to be processed by payroll.

Note: You may have to add this type of earnings to your earnings table.

Do not touch the COBOL in Ben Admin. The plan you need to implement is easily accomplished using the above steps. It's really not much different from any other plan; it's just specific to your company. If you need to, run SQR's after Ben admin, don't change to COBOL!

☞ QUESTION 96

Human Resources Module PeopleSoft vs. SAP

I looking for an alternative to ultimately become an Oracle E-Biz/Fusion lemming. Since I'm running PeopleSoft Human Resources and SAP for everything else and I'm thinking about migrating from PeopleSoft to SAP HR module. I'm in a single application platform.

What are pros vs. cons on each module?

Does my planned move make sense?

✍ ANSWER

You should wait to see what Oracle's migration plans turn out to be. If their commitments are true, it'll be 5 years before you need to make a decision. By that time, both SAP and Oracle will have mature methodologies to get you off of PeopleTools). I'm assuming that you're on PSFT in the first place because at one time you found it to be better than SAP's HR.

If you want to see a module/module comparison, contact your account manager from SAP and PeopleSoft. They'll both be happy to send you their marketing material as to why their products are better.

☞ **QUESTION 97**

Salary Increase after MASS CHANGE - 8.8

In Mexico minimum salary wages change on Jan 01 2005. Mass change is no longer working for release 8.8.

I need some help or guidelines as to how to change the COMPRATE for those employees that make the minimum wage. The change has to insert a new row on JOB effective dates as 1-1-6 with the new amount.

Just in case anyone else has operations in Mexico here are the new minimum wages:

    Zone A -- from 52.24 to 46.80
    Zone B -- 43.73 45.35
    Zone C -- 42.11 44.05

Ideally I would like to see it done through the application by end-users.
We are a hotel chain with 14 locations in Mexico where each location administers the employees under their roof.

We have 14 end-users that would do 'row insert' to several employees (from 10 to 300). It is in the larger hotels that automating the process will be of much benefit.

How do I configure the changes?

✍ ANSWER

If you just want to insert the job rows manually, you'll need to update three tables that must always be in sync.

JOB
JOB_JR
COMPENSATION

The best option though is to build an application engine or SQR program that performs the operation for JOB, JOB_JR and COMP.

An alternative would be to solve the issue through the use of Group Increases:

1- Define Group (and Group Security);
2- Create & approve Group Budget;
3- Assign & approve individual increases;
4- Approve Salary Plan;
5- Load increases;

☞ **QUESTION 98**

PeopleSoft Gross up

I know how to gross up a check but I cannot figure out the calculation it is using. I've tried doing an off cycle check for $500, calculating it and adding the tax to it to see if it matches what PeopleSoft comes up with for the Gross up amount. I always calculate something lower.

What is the algorithm or formula PeopleSoft uses to Gross up?

✍ **ANSWER**

Gross up is a function of how taxes operate in each country.

I will give an example being used in Mexico with Global Payroll. While the way to accomplish it is quite lengthy to replicate here, in essence what can be done is:

Take net (base net) and multiply by 1.6 (top net);
Add base net and top net and divide by 2 (mid net);
Calculate taxes on top net;
Compare result with mid net;
If higher then mid net becomes base net;
Add new base net and top net and divide by 2 (mid net);
And then repeat these if lower; then mid net becomes top net;
Add base net and new top net and divide by 2 (mid net);
And then repeat;
End when difference is less than X;

☞ QUESTION **99**

HCM 8.9 Upgrade or New Implementation

I am wondering if any of you are considering an upgrade or new implementation to HCM 8.9. If so, what is the time frame and what in HCM 8.9 would convince you to make this move?

✍ ANSWER

I strongly suggest you to do a "New Implementation" to 8.8. It all depends on what release you are on now, but so many things changed from 7.5 to 8.9 that making an upgrade will take a lot of time and effort. I am not saying that a new installation is trivial, but it is much better. It also presents a great opportunity to bring back to 'standard' things that have changed.

As for the time consideration, there are so many factors that it is very hard to say but a ball park time would be 3 to 12 months.

☞ QUESTION 100

Multiple Pay Entities

I have always been advised by previous colleagues that having more than one pay entity 'open' concurrently is unwise. For example, we have a weekly and monthly payroll and the payroll guys need to work on both at the same time.

Is it correct that having multiple payrolls open is bad?

Are there any restrictions or management considerations?

✍ ANSWER

Actually. The only issue would be that any employee in both pay entities would be suspended in the second, if the first is open.

Otherwise there are no issues from GSC.

INDEX

Attention SAP Experts

Have you ever considered writing a book in your area of SAP? Equity Press is the leading provider of knowledge products in SAP applications consulting, development, and support. If you have a manuscript or an idea of a manuscript, we'd love to help you get it published!

Please send your manuscript or manuscript ideas to jim@sapcookbook.com – we'll help you turn your dream into a reality.

Or mail your inquiries to:

Equity Press Manuscripts
BOX 706
Riverside, California
92502

Tel (951)788-0810
Fax (951)788-0812

50% Off your next
SAPCOOKBOOK order

If you plan of placing an order for 10 or more books from www.sapcookbook.com you qualify for volume discounts. Please send an email to books@sapcookbook.com or phone 951-788-0810 to place your order.

You can also fax your orders to 951-788-0812 .

Interview books are great for cross-training

In the new global economy, the more you know the better. The sharpest consultants are doing everything they can to pick up more than one functional area of SAP. Each of the following Certification Review / Interview Question books provides an excellent starting point for your module learning and investigation. These books get you started like no other book can – by providing you the information that you really need to know, and fast.

SAPCOOKBOOK Interview Questions, Answers, and Explanations

ABAP - SAP ABAP Certification Review: SAP ABAP Interview Questions, Answers, and Explanations

SD - SAP SD Interview Questions, Answers, and Explanations

Security - SAP Security: SAP Security Essentials

HR - mySAP HR Interview Questions, Answers, and Explanations: SAP HR Certification Review

BW - SAP BW Ultimate Interview Questions, Answers, and Explanations: SAW BW Certification Review

- SAP SRM Interview Questions Answers and Explanations

Basis - SAP Basis Certification Questions: Basis Interview Questions, Answers, and Explanations

MM - SAP MM Certification and Interview Questions: SAP MM Interview Questions, Answers, and Explanations

SAP BW Ultimate Interview Questions, Answers, and Explanations

Key Topics Include:

- The most important BW settings to know
- BW tables and transaction code quick references
- Certification Examination Questions
- Extraction, Modeling and Configuration
- Transformations and Administration
- Performance Tuning, Tips & Tricks, and FAQ
- Everything a BW resource needs to know before an interview

mySAP HR Interview Questions, Answers, and Explanations

Key topics include:

- The most important HR settings to know
- mySAP HR Administration tables and transaction code quick references
- SAP HR Certification Examination Questions
- Org plan, Compensation, Year End, Wages, and Taxes
- User Management, Transport System, Patches, and Upgrades
- Benefits, Holidays, Payroll, and Infotypes
- Everything an HR resource needs to know before an interview

SAP SRM Interview Questions, Answers, and Explanations

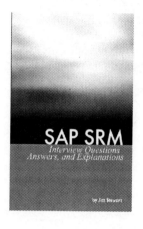

Key Topics Include:

- The most important SRM Configuration to know
- Common EBP Implementation Scenarios
- Purchasing Document Approval Processes
- Supplier Self Registration and Self Service (SUS)
- Live Auctions and Bidding Engine, RFX Processes (LAC)
- Details for Business Intelligence and Spend Analysis
- EBP Technical and Troubleshooting Information

SAP MM Interview Questions, Answers, and Explanations

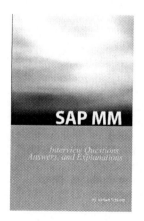

- The most important MM Configuration to know
- Common MM Implementation Scenarios
- MM Certification Exam Questions
- Consumption Based Planning
- Warehouse Management
- Material Master Creation and Planning
- Purchasing Document Inforecords

SAP SD Interview Questions, Answers, and Explanations

- The most important SD settings to know
- SAP SD administration tables and transaction code quick references
- SAP SD Certification Examination Questions
- Sales Organization and Document Flow Introduction
- Partner Procedures, Backorder Processing, Sales BOM
- Backorder Processing, Third Party Ordering, Rebates and Refunds
- Everything an SD resource needs to know before an interview

SAP Basis Interview Questions, Answers, and Explanations

- The most important Basis settings to know
- Basis Administration tables and transaction code quick references
- Certification Examination Questions
- Oracle database, UNIX, and MS Windows Technical Information
- User Management, Transport System, Patches, and Upgrades
- Backup and Restore, Archiving, Disaster Recover, and Security
- Everything a Basis resource needs to know before an interview

SAP Security Essentials

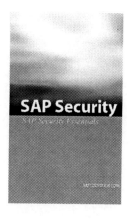

- Finding Audit Critical Combinations
- Authentication, Transaction Logging, and Passwords
- Roles, Profiles, and User Management
- ITAR, DCAA, DCMA, and Audit Requirements
- The most important security settings to know
- Security Tuning, Tips & Tricks, and FAQ
- Transaction code list and table name references

SAP Workflow Interview Questions, Answers, and Explanations

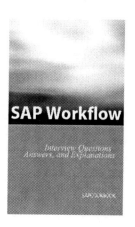

- Database Updates and Changing the Standard
- List Processing, Internal Tables, and ALV Grid Control
- Dialog Programming, ABAP Objects
- Data Transfer, Basis Administration
- ABAP Development reference updated for 2006!
- Everything an ABAP resource needs to know before an interview

Lightning Source UK Ltd.
Milton Keynes UK
01 February 2010

149404UK00001B/92/A